A PLACE IN THE
CURRANT BUN

A PLACE IN THE CURRANT BUN

JO HAMILTON

authorHOUSE®

AuthorHouse™ UK Ltd.
500 Avebury Boulevard
Central Milton Keynes, MK9 2BE
www.authorhouse.co.uk
Phone: 08001974150

First published by AuthorHouse 9/30/2010

ISBN: 978-1-4520-8531-9 (sc)

This book is printed on acid-free paper.

In memory of Ann Cookson (1938 – 2008)

A big thanks to Dad, Rob, Mick, Tom, Alan, Carol B, Mick B, Chris, Mal, Jean, Dave, and Mel for being the best mates anyone could wish for.

Contents

Introduction

Anyone who decides to relocate abroad generally carries out copious research beforehand and reads whatever book on the subject that they can lay their hands on. I was no different. In amongst the 'serious' and very useful books I read on buying property in Spain, tax in Spain and working in Spain were several anecdotal 'dos and don'ts' publications and those detailing other people's trials and tribulations. The one thing the latter category had in common was that they all contained an element of humour – ranging from the mildly amusing to the absolutely hilarious. Of course none of these put me off in the slightest. I imagined that, in the same situation, I too would laugh, shake my head, and accept the quirks of the move with the same laidback *joie de vivre*. How wrong could I have been?

This book is for anyone contemplating a similar move; especially those who have not yet retired. I would not dream of giving specific advice (all people's situations are different, and the rules in the country, or region, of choice will vary), but I may raise issues for some people that they have overlooked. Before you spend a significant amount of your hard-earned money on any foreign property, take just a few hours out of your life to read my story. It might just make some people readjust their plans, ask some searching questions, or have a complete rethink. The rest can just have a laugh at my expense and I wish them success and the best of luck for the future.

This is not a rulebook; all legal information should be checked out with properly qualified professionals, and all decisions should be carefully made to take into account your own circumstances. I acted on information that did not always turn out to be accurate, and was given conflicting advice many times. I am sure that I still don't know the truth surrounding some issues, but I have emerged from the ordeal with a very different outlook on life and a tougher, more confident, attitude towards risk taking and the trying of new things. Many tears have been shed during the process and my relationships with my loved ones sorely tested, some to breaking point. Tread carefully and know yourself is the best advice I can give you.

I am sure some expats will read this book and object to every sentence, some will dismiss me as a whiner and others will empathise with every word.

"Get back to the UK – people like you only have a shelf life of two years anyway," I can hear them shouting now. I do not intend to offend anyone and I am sure there are many happy expats in Spain, but there are hundreds, if not thousands, who are very unhappy. This book is to help you to avoid making the mistakes that many others and I have already made. I have changed the names of everyone involved and I have specifically sought permission from the woman I call 'Janet' who had a particularly horrific time. She is happy for her story to be told, and I thank her for allowing me to include the details in this book.

What you will read is simply my account of what happened in my five years of living in Spain – and, at times, if I could have turned the clock back, I sure as hell would have. I used to be an organised individual and I really believed that I had covered all my bases. Unfortunately I failed to factor in my own vulnerabilities (actually I wasn't aware of them until they manifested themselves, and by that time it was far too late). I was totally unprepared for the unexpected and, for a while, my life ended up derailed and chaotic instead of fun and relaxed. This story is real, and it really is not funny!

To understand how I progressed from being an excited expat to a mental wreck, and from a mental wreck to a relaxed individual who really couldn't care less what happened next, all in the space of five years, we first have to take a step back to 2004 and an unwise and regrettable visit to an overseas property exhibition ...

January 2004 –
There Has To Be More To Life Than This

If I'd known at the outset what 2006 was going to be like, I just simply would not have bothered seeing in the New Year. Instead I would have gone to bed at the end of 2005 and stayed there until 2007. Or, even worse, I would have cancelled the plans for 2006 and stuck with my old life. Having not been blessed with the gift of foresight I did neither, and barrelled along into the New Year full of hope and eagerness; feelings that were destined to change places with anxiety and despair with monotonous regularity.

Tony, my partner, had said that 2006 was going to be *our year*. Of course he meant this in a positive way and I believed him, it sounded great, but the reality was to be scarily different from the expectation and promise of what we had planned for ourselves. I have never liked roller coaster rides but this virtual 'roller coaster of life' was destined to be far more distasteful than any real ride I had ever experienced. The biggest problem was that it was more or less all my own doing, and my friends will tell you that I have never been very good at admitting that I have screwed up.

The whole situation came about mainly because I was sick of my workplace and even sicker of being at the disposal of an organisation that I no longer respected. Having been in the same profession for over 20 years I doubted that what I did made any real difference. My promotion prospects had run out, I was 42, bored, and going nowhere. On a daily basis I robotically reported in and listened to the same old depressed grumblings from colleagues stuck in the same rut as me. The situation was getting me down. I lost count of the number of times my concentration would drift off as I thought that there had to be more to life than *this*... Faced with another 20 years of much the same I eventually decided that enough was enough and that it was time to try something else. If I stayed I would go crazy (I ended up crazy anyway so financially I probably would have been better off staying put).

Anyway, I feel that the presenters of 'Holiday Home' TV shows must share some of the blame for the horrible situation we eventually found ourselves in. There they are in our homes at the end of a hard day's graft, showing us marvellous properties in sunny climates at prices that apparently are a fraction of what you would pay for a flat in rain-soaked Manchester. They make it look so easy that you would think anyone could do it. I did think anyone could do it, and what is even worse I thought I could do it – and I did! I dragged Tony into it too and unintentionally stressed out my dad for good measure at a time when he should have been enjoying his retirement.

I knew plenty of people who were also dreaming of a place in the sun, but no one ever did anything about it (that rut is just so safe and comfortable that the majority of us do nothing to get out of it). Then I decided, in January 2004, that Tony and I would go to an overseas property exhibition at Manchester's G-Mex, 'just to have a look'. Yeah right! Have you ever known a woman to go shopping and come back empty-handed?

Tony was not enthralled and I dragged him around the exhibition hall in the same way that you would drag a petulant seven-year-old around a supermarket. We were pestered from the moment we entered the place. Which country were we interested in; how much money did we have readily available; when could we come out to view; what was our telephone number? Tony began to lose his cool and just wanted to get out. We resorted to approaching stands when all the representatives were already talking to people; grabbing their brochures and then disappearing into the crowd. When snared, I gave out a false telephone number. The hard-sell style really put us off and we were fed up and just about to leave when we were half-heartedly approached by a representative from the agent from which we were eventually to buy. In contrast to the others, he looked as fed up as we felt and he did not ask for our details. He simply showed us some plans of the size of property we could expect to get for our money, gave us his card and wished us well.

Over the next couple of days the phone never stopped ringing. Reps making follow-up calls had somehow managed to track me down even though I had given most of them the wrong number. This was quite alarming and most annoying, partly because I had not succeeded with my deception and partly because they had hardly given us time to think the matter through. I know that reps think it is important to get to potential customers before someone else does, but surely they realise that we Brits really dislike being hassled, and that buying a property requires some thought? I got rid of all of them as politely as I could, but several of them bugged me for weeks afterwards.

The plan, at this stage, was simply to purchase a holiday home as a place to escape to in the short term and as an investment in the long term. I was also conscious of the need to select an area which was sufficiently popular for resale to be relatively easy should the need arise. I specifically asked these questions later on and was assured that resale was easy and we would have no problems getting a property off our hands when it had served its purpose. I spent a lot of time looking through the brochures. We had only collected those covering the Costa Blanca south as my research on the Internet had convinced me that the area was ideally placed for regular cheap flights, close enough for long weekend breaks and, most importantly, affordable. As I was only looking for a holiday home, the search was narrowed even further to apartments with two bedrooms, and we wanted it to be only a short walk to the coast. I also knew from watching the TV programmes that we would have to go for 'off-plan' as it would be financially more comfortable for us to spread the cost of the purchase over several months. The same programmes had also given me the impression that 'off-plan' properties would be worth more by the time they were completed, as the market would rise during the building process. I also knew that I would have to add approximately 11% to cover all the taxes and fees. The budget was set and the deposit was available.

Having selected five properties with floor plans which were attractive and within budget, and having exhausted not only the property choices within the brochures but also those on the respective websites, I contacted the man who had not annoyed me to arrange an inspection trip with his company.

Prior to setting off, and being what the property companies would call a 'serious buyer', I used a broker to buy sufficient euros to cover the deposit at times and rates that were to our advantage; though I now think that that was not strictly necessary as the company from which we were buying did offer a very competitive exchange rate. I also set up my own Spanish bank account with very professional assistance from the staff of the Solbank. This suited my needs more than the bank recommended by the agent because with this particular Solbank account I could check the balance online from the UK and also carry out my own transfers. Not all Spanish banks offer an online service in English. In my naiveté it seems I was already taking far too much control of my own situation; it is not something the property companies like.

The inspection trip was subsidised by the selling agents, and ours looked after us marvellously during our four days in the Torrevieja/southern Costa Blanca area. Fortunately, Tony and I have always been very lucky when it comes to meeting decent people, and this experience was no exception. The couple that picked us up from the airport, showed us around the show homes and introduced us to the area, became and remain friends, though my attitude towards the agency they worked for was not to be so consistent.

Our guides' names were Pauline and Phil and we had been allocated a minibus to be shared with another couple who were supposed to be looking to buy in the same price bracket and who had indicated that they had similar requirements to ours. This is common practice, no doubt it is cost-effective to fill a bus and pack in more customers, but I was glad that there were only the four of us as the other couple turned out to be what the property companies would call 'time wasters', on a cheap weekend away. (It doesn't take long to become familiar with the terms these agents use to categorise their clients.) However, as our guides couldn't accuse the other couple of being 'time wasters', we spent valuable hours driving miles to look at properties in which none of us was remotely interested.

Pauline and Phil's technique was similar to that of the chap from the G-Mex and once again there was no pressure. Their attitude was that we were spending a lot of money so it had to be right and therefore our ideal property, when we found it, would sell itself. This was the correct approach as far as we were concerned. Any attempt at hard sell on their part would have terminated our search very quickly. It would be fair to say though that four days is not very long to find an ideal property in an area with which you are unfamiliar and I soon discovered that the brochure had been a little deceptive. Three properties from my selection were unsuitable simply because, despite what it said in the description, they were in the middle of nowhere (ten minutes to the beach was definitely an exaggeration on their part – perhaps they meant by Concorde?). We therefore looked at several properties in remote locations before we settled on an apartment in an area called Los Altos and a design known at the time as a 'Granada II'. The development benefited from sea views; it was only a short walk to the beach and the presence of a couple of commercial centres and a supermarket confirmed it to be our ideal location. I looked at the site plan and reserved a top floor apartment on the corner of a block with an uninterrupted sea view and a private roof terrace. Tony went outside for a fag (he doesn't do decisions). The estimated date of completion was June 2005, give or take several months either side. It was slightly over budget, but I felt that the position it was in justified the extra cost.

Los Altos is a great spot for a holiday home and we felt that the property would have decent rental potential as not only were there plenty of English bars and restaurants nearby but also small Spanish towns and markets were within easy reach. It felt like we had got the best of both worlds. We were also informed that a large new hospital was to be opened in the summer of 2006, only a couple of kilometres away, so if we decided to take on a long let there were likely to be plenty of takers.

We returned to the hotel to do the paperwork and hand over a deposit; the remaining payment terms were clearly laid out and nicely spread over the following 18 months. So that was it, mission accomplished, holiday home in the sun in the bag. I was satisfied with the transaction, had made an informed decision and was more than pleased with the treatment and support we had received from our guides. If we had left it at that, things may have been smoother in the long run but we had both been seduced by the laidback lifestyle of our guides. They had jumped off the UK treadmill and survived. Perhaps we could too.

On the flight home Tony surprised me by saying how much he had enjoyed himself and how he thought we could do a job together like our new friends. They had seemed so happy at work and had told us that there was 'always a need for new couples on the vans'. They offered to put in a good word for us if we ever fancied applying. Apparently the fact that we had bought from the company would also count in our favour. Strangely enough I had been thinking exactly the same thing as Tony so clearly we were both enthusiastic about the idea. It was therefore, at this early stage, that a new seed was sown – the possibility of a complete change, a full relocation, and new jobs. If only we had known what lay ahead of us. Ignorance really is bliss.

Back To Reality

At the time of our discontent at home, both of us had well-paid, safe, supervisory-level jobs in local government, but the tedium, constant rule-changing and political correctness was getting to us both. Staff didn't seem to want to carry out even their core tasks without arguing about whether it was their turn to do X, Y or Z, whilst the management droned on about 'the way forward' without us ever seeming to go anywhere.

Over the years the pressure of work had taken its toll on my health and I had been on medication to prevent panic attacks for a couple of years. I was also gaining weight at an alarming rate and suffering the aches and pains associated with a largely sedentary lifestyle. Tony was a heavy smoker with high blood pressure and high cholesterol and the health of his mum, who lived a four-hour drive away from us, was becoming an increasing cause for concern, requiring him to make more and more visits. After a lengthy discussion, we felt that the time had finally come for us to start leading simpler lives and for us to feel more satisfied with what we already had. We wanted our health to improve and to have more time for the people who meant a lot to us and we were both willing to take the risks that were necessary in order to achieve it all. That's what we thought at the time anyway.

In the meantime we went back to work and back to *normal* (whatever that is). We hadn't told many people of our plans to buy abroad in case we came back empty-handed, and it was several more months before we told anyone, including our own families, that our plans had reached a completely new level.

In June 2004 I had a hysterectomy followed by three months off work. For the first time in 23 years I had a significant period of time to myself outside of the workplace and I became a different person. Free from the petty squabbling of staff and the bizarre decisions of management, I relaxed and stopped swearing. I wasn't on the verge of anger all the time. I stopped taking my 'happy pills', lost weight and felt much healthier. I dreaded going back.

Much of my time off work was spent brushing up on my night school Spanish and planning ahead for all the disasters that I could foresee. The more we discussed the move the more it seemed like the right thing to do; neither one of us wavered from the moment the decision was made. Neither of us was naive enough to think that it would all go exactly according to plan but, being a control freak, I was fairly sure that I could get it pretty close to the ideal if I thought it through well enough.

Shortly before the end of my period of recuperation Tony decided it would do us good to have a long weekend in Spain to check on the progress of the apartment and obtain our NIE numbers whilst we were at it. (This was mistake number one – if we hadn't taken this particular trip things still would have been OK, but we did take it and I went on to make the one decision that I now sorely regret.)

Anyway, the NIE number is an identification number for foreigners in Spain. You need one of these to complete a property purchase, buy a car or to work (amongst other things). Obtaining such a number is relatively easy but not particularly convenient. We were taken by the agent's representative to a government building in Alicante and were standing in line by 5:30am in order to be sure of obtaining a cloakroom ticket to get into the building when it opened at 9am. At the time we went, only 120 people per day were allowed in for processing. Unfortunately, our visit also coincided with some sort of amnesty that Spain was giving to illegal workers from North Africa. They had one last chance to make themselves legal before being chucked out. We therefore found ourselves in a huge crowd consisting mainly of swarthy men in hooded garments who were not well practised in the British art of queuing. Luckily, our agents were very familiar with the system and by 1pm we had the precious number that many people, applying at other venues, would have to wait a couple of weeks to be allocated with. It is now normal practice for agents or solicitors to charge up to €120 per person for this NIE number service but, luckily for us, when we went it was free.

The progress of the apartment was well on schedule. At the building site in Los Altos we were surprised to discover that, even though it was still a year before completion, the shell of the block was up and we could see that our apartment was in as good a position as the site plan had indicated. This was a relief as we had heard from another couple that their property had a massive pylon in front of it that had not been marked on the plan they had been given to view. We were to discover other pitfalls associated with off-plan buying, but nobody will fall over themselves to warn you when there is a property to sell. The fees paid by the builders to the agents are huge, and many agency staff are employed on a commission-only basis so there are clearly conflicts of interest involved which are not to the benefit of the potential purchaser.

However, it was during another look around the show apartment that we realised that whilst the apartment was ideal for a holiday home it was probably too small for permanent occupancy. A readjustment needed to be made if we were to go ahead with a complete move. Several options were discussed and it was agreed that we would spend our remaining days looking at larger properties, suitable for our relocation plans. In the time we had available we only saw one villa that we both loved, but it was too remote to be practical for anyone needing to work, so it was discounted and we thought no more about it. Instead we arranged to meet Pauline and Phil from the property company for a farewell drink as we were leaving the next day. This was mistake number two and it had a direct impact on what subsequently happened.

Our rendezvous was a café near a waterfall feature across from the marina in Torrevieja. When we told our friends what we had been up to, they offered to take us to a town called Los Montesinos where some lovely finca-style villas were being built. They had reserved one for themselves and said that this particular development was not yet in any of the brochures. We were not too familiar with the area inland so we would never have discovered it for ourselves, even though it turned out to be only 20 minutes from Los Altos. They were eager to show us where they would be living, so we took them up on the offer and headed off in their car.

The villas were well designed and had lovely views over lemon groves and salt lakes, and we were both immediately impressed with the 'Spanishness' of Los Montesinos. The expat community had already infiltrated the town on a fairly small scale but it had managed to retain its identity and had not given in to the English-speaking presence in a big way. We were also glad to hear that the majority of the villas had been reserved for full-time residents rather than holidaymakers. This, we hoped, would give some stability to the community and believed that that would be a good thing. (In time I came to realise that physical stability does not guarantee a stress-free living environment – unknown to me at the time I made my fateful decision; behind curtains, roller shutters, iron bars, triple-locking doors and mosquito screens all over Spain, and particularly it seemed on the Costa Blanca, there were expats going crackers.)

Pauline said it would be great to have us as neighbours and we said we would give it some thought. The next day, in a spur of the moment decision, we decided to go back on our own to weigh up the situation. Tony loved the atmosphere of the town and I liked the fact that it had not become an English-speaking ghetto. The villa had a great layout and the plots were generous enough for a private pool. We asked the show home representative for a copy of the site plan, which gave some indication of which plots were still for sale. The row where our friends' plot was situated was completely reserved and anyway the completion dates were far too early for our plans so, much to Tony's amazement, I asked to reserve a corner plot facing some farmland, with the building completion date estimated at September 2005. The reservation could be held for 24 hours. (Two years later I would go through hell and beat myself up for making that snap decision, but at the time it seemed like the right thing to do.) We went into the village to have a brew and talk things over. I told Tony I would sell my flat in Manchester to finance the purchase, as I really wanted to commit myself to the move, and in the meantime I could remortgage it to cover some of the staged payments. With that problem apparently settled we rang our friends, told them the news and offered to let them take credit for the sale. They were delighted, and during the next couple of hours we did a lot of scurrying about with bits of paperwork between the show house and their office. When we got back to Los Montesinos to pick up our hire car we found that it had been chained into the town square and a load of tables had been set up around it. This brought forth a few expletives from all of us, but eventually we managed to liberate it in time to get back to the airport for our flight home. I'd been to the Costa Blanca twice and bought a property each time. Tony was still stunned when we got on the plane. I don't think he ever really believed that I was serious about moving – well he now knew differently!

Clearly we now had two Spanish properties on our hands and we really didn't need them both, so we decided that we would hold on to the apartment and try to rent it out to holidaymakers full-time in order to give us a small income and something to do in the short term. We would sell it on when it had served its purpose or when we needed to free up the money. It had never been our intention to have more than one Spanish property, so the sell-off option was likely to happen sooner rather than later. I didn't envisage this being a problem. If you believe the holiday home programmes, selling property abroad is easier than at home, isn't it – aren't there thousands of people out there just dying to buy? All I can say now is, don't believe what you see on TV. Most of the shows are repeats and the property market in Spain has definitely changed!

Planning Ahead

The return to work after my operation was a shock to my system and I found it hard to settle back into the old rut. I had received no return-to-work plan from my manager and was back on my 'panic attack' medication within a month. The only thing that kept me going was the knowledge that it was no longer the only avenue now open to me. My ability to tolerate petty behaviour was much reduced and my discomfort within the workplace confirmed the decision to move. Ironically, in order to make the transition to Spain more financially viable, I worked masses of overtime to build up our savings, but I was sure that the sacrifice was going to be worth it. We planned out exactly when we would put the Manchester flat on the market and organised alternative accommodation in case it sold quickly. My renewed optimism for the future never left me and I never once imagined that it would not work out marvellously.

There was no opportunity for me to hedge my bets and preserve my employment in any way; a sabbatical would not have worked and I was really too old to be asking for a career break so I would have to take the chance, bite the bullet and just resign. Tony on the other hand was 57 and his health was deteriorating so we decided that it would be sensible, and fair, for him to apply for early retirement. At the time in the UK, 50 was the age at which a person became eligible to apply for early retirement, so we knew he would easily qualify. We also mistakenly believed that his application would be favourably considered, as he was a hard worker with very little sickness absence on record. You would think an employer would look after loyal staff – well *we* did. In the meantime we started sorting out issues connected with the move.

As the apartment was supposed to be ready before the villa, and we intended to rent it out, we wanted to get it up and running as quickly as possible. We did not want to buy a lot of furniture in Spain as we already had a lot of stuff at home and I believed that it would help the transition if we had some familiar things around us. The Eurotunnel was cheaper than the ferry and we intended to save money by doing our own removals; we didn't mind the drive, as it was all part of the adventure. A Luton van would be ideal and we would do a second trip later with the furniture for the villa when it was ready.

We tried to price-up van hire and were surprised to find that many companies would not allow their vehicles out of the UK (or if they did they only allowed them to venture into France). Eventually we found a company that would allow their vehicle to be taken to Spain, but we had to pay extra and hire a van that was larger than the one we really needed. This meant that the plan had to be readjusted to make the best use of the cost of the van, so we decided that we would have to rough it with very little furniture in Manchester and take everything in one go. It also meant that we had to book ourselves onto the more expensive freight Eurotunnel rather than the regular one because the van no longer came within the allowed limits. Fate was already stacking up a barrelful of laughs for us without us even knowing.

In the meantime, having assessed our possessions and come to the conclusion that we had far too much 'stuff' that we neither used nor needed, I began selling items on an Internet auction site which netted us in excess of £3000. This comfortably covered the cost of the removal van, toll charges and fuel from Manchester to Spain, and de-junked our cupboards at the same time.

After that it was a waiting game until the apartment in Los Altos was ready. I had been told that I would receive a letter and that I should then contact the agent to arrange 'moving in'. In the meantime I had to battle to get our inspection trip money refunded. This should have happened automatically upon our return in February 2004. Those who bought with this particular agent got their money back and those who didn't, did not. However I had been warned that if I did not receive it automatically and failed to chase it up, someone from the sales office would pocket the money. It took four requests over three months to get it back. Six months later the company lost a cheque of mine for €65000 in respect of a payment on the villa and you can be sure that they were rather more swift to ask me for a replacement. They also added to their e-mail a 'friendly' warning that if it reached them too late I might incur a penalty from the Spanish builder. Such double standards were a taste of things to come.

Then, things started to go wrong with the master plan. Tony's initial application for early retirement was refused. His mum's health, which was already poor, went into a steady decline and he in turn had to make more regular trips to South Wales from Manchester. This was taking its toll on his health with the result that he was finding it harder to recover from the demands of shift working. He resubmitted his application several months later on compassionate grounds, but this time not only was he met with the same response i.e. refusal, he was also advised that references to his ability to cope with the shifts might be regarded as a capability issue rather than one worthy of consideration for early retirement. Until this point we had believed that Tony was a valued and respected member of staff and that they would have at least sat down with him and discussed his situation. The 'caring employer' however was beginning to start showing its true colours.

We discussed the rejection at length and decided that when we were ready we would both just resign. We had calculated that we could move over in January 2006 and so planned to time everything so that we could leave together at the end of December 2005. We would live off our savings, and as a last resort I would cash in my premium bonds to keep us going until we found work.

In February 2005 I put the Manchester flat up for sale. The market was dead, and we only had three viewers in several months. This caused me some concern but we felt it would come good in the end. I dropped the price and changed estate agent but to no avail.

In August 2005 I received a letter from the builders advising me that the Spanish apartment was ready. I contacted the agent through which I was buying and said we would like to take possession during the second week in September. I was told this would be fine, so Tony and I swapped shifts and booked annual leave, a flight for me, and the removal van. I would fly over, do the legal stuff and take possession of the keys whilst Tony and my dad would drive over with the furniture. That meant three uncomfortable months in the Manchester flat, but it was all going to be worth it. I spoke to the agent again to confirm that we had booked everything and would be ready for the hand-over of the keys as previously arranged. To my surprise she said I had not made any arrangements and that they could not fit me in, I was not a priority and they were too busy. I protested that I had followed their instructions to the letter and that they had to honour the arrangement. She then said that they had not told me that the property was ready so as far as they were concerned I could not have the keys. Being a very organised person I had the letter in front of me and proceeded to read it out, only to be interrupted with "That is not our letter, that is a letter from the builder" – "I know, the builder says it is ready" – "It is not ready if *we* haven't told you its ready" – "But it is" – "No it is not, *we* will decide when it is ready *not* the builder." So much for customer relations. It seemed that the process was to be dealt with at their convenience, not ours.

I had several more irate conversations with this snotty individual, who made it quite plain that I was getting far too involved in my own property purchase. I was told quite bluntly that I should not be making any travel or removal arrangements without clearing it with them first and that they handled completion dates, not the builder. I had responded to the wrong letter so as far as they were concerned I was being totally unreasonable. Clearly all that was required of me was to hand over large wodges of hard-earned cash at the allotted times and they would do the rest. I had mistakenly assumed that I had an interest in the process, when in fact I was simply an irritating detail.

Eventually I lost patience, took the matter further and still had to make a complete nuisance of myself (which I don't like doing even though I can do it very well). Very reluctantly they fitted us in and oh boy was I left in no doubt how inconvenient it all was. *(Well excuse me!)*

September 2005 –
Welcome To Spain (Not) 1

The appointments with the solicitor, the translator and the notary went very smoothly and I was very satisfied with the finish on the apartment. The site manager came, checked that everything was OK, and attended to the snags immediately. This was not what I had been led to believe would happen. I had heard that snagging was a nightmare but it seems on this occasion at least I had 'gotten lucky' as they say in American films.

On the other hand, shopping for the fixtures and fittings turned out to be a bizarre experience, and one that I was destined to have to repeat with the villa. The company through which I purchased my properties offered a choice of 'gift' to its customers (I suspect it is factored into the price); this was either a furniture pack or a €2100 voucher to spend on fixtures. These had to be obtained from their recommended store (which habitually overcharges for mediocre goods). I opted for the voucher for two reasons: because the furniture packs are comprised of tacky furniture and because we had enough stuff already. As most brand new Spanish property comes as a shell without so much as an oven and hob or a ceiling rose I intended to cash in my voucher on light fixtures and kitchen appliances – the very things that we were not going to be bringing with us. I had a list of essential items and was happy to discover that fitting was included in the service. What I was totally unprepared for was the minimal amount of time I was to be allocated to spend the voucher. The procedure was that the 'moving in team' representative would pick you up, take you to the store and take a ticket in a similar routine experienced at a supermarket deli counter. You would then browse the store whilst waiting for your number to come up. When your number appeared you would be allocated a salesperson from the store, who basically expected you to have already made your mind up whilst browsing. They jot down the codes of the items as you say "I'll have one of these and four of these", then they take you back to the desk and tell you if you have overspent or if you need to very quickly think of something else to use up your voucher. You cannot split a voucher and come back another day and you get very little thinking time. No one would normally pick fixtures and fittings for a new home in less than 30 minutes, but there is a subliminal pressure applied so that you do not dawdle and make things difficult for everybody. I managed to kit out the kitchen, choose all the light fittings and bathroom fitments such as mirrors and towel rails in the allotted time. To this day I still hate those light fittings!

Thankfully Tony and Dad arrived safely with our worldly goods and with the help of Dave, the son of Pauline and Phil, we spent the next two days hauling everything up three flights of stairs. The apartment came with rooftop storage and that is where we stashed the items we intended to take to the villa. At the end of the two days I vowed that I would never ask my dad to lift another box in his life!

Inevitably during the process the few residents who were already in spotted us. The greeting we got from one happy soul was "Have you been burgled yet?" Marvellous! This harbinger of doom gleefully went on to tell us that everyone who had just moved in had been burgled and that it was bound to happen to us; apparently one chap had even had his dirty underwear stolen. Whilst we were emptying the van we were dressed casually bordering on downright scruffy so I did not fear for the safety of my washing. My complacency however was misplaced.

As we had to get the van back to the UK (no one we contacted did one way van hire) we were only going to spend three nights in the apartment before setting off back. Two of my closest friends, John and Alex, were then arriving for a free holiday and to test-drive the apartment from the viewpoint of a customer. They turned up in smart designer gear and were a complete contrast to us in appearance. We would overlap by one night and decided to celebrate. John and Alex had brought two bottles of champagne for the occasion and we prepared a buffet and installed ourselves on the balcony for a good booze up. The doorbell (one of my hasty acquisitions) played 28 different tunes and unfortunately my dad (an ex rugby player) knew unofficial words to at least one of them. Several hours later, following numerous drunken renditions of 'The hair on her dickey dido', we went to bed.

The next morning Tony and my dad decided that they had enjoyed themselves so much that we could stay for one more night and still get the van back on time. The husband of the doom-monger then showed up and asked us if we had heard all the noise in the night? We said no, why? He told us that yobs and druggies from the 'front' had been on the urbanisation (development or estate), making a noise, singing songs and that there had even been two gunshots. A woman in the next block was scared to come out of her apartment and had stayed up all night because she was so worried she couldn't sleep. She was considering going home. I was beginning to wonder what we had bought into – the place was being made to sound like a war zone.

After he'd gone we realised that it was probably us they had heard and that the 'gunshots' were the champagne corks popping. It illustrated how an incident could be exaggerated and the fear of God put into someone for no reason. I dismissed the new neighbour as being an over sensitive, grumpy old nutter. To be honest, I hadn't been particularly concerned about security until Mr Happy came a-calling. The apartment came with a built-in safe (which was a surprise) but its keys had not been handed over during the moving-in process (which was not a surprise). The agents now had their money and were not interested in assisting us to find out who had them so it remained temporarily out of use. I had been advised to have security grilles fitted to the windows but had also been told not to buy them from builder or the agent as they "Mark them up and rip you off". Dave knew someone who quoted a good price and so the grilles had been ordered but would not be ready for a week so John and Alex had agreed to stay in on the day they were to be fitted.

We prepared the van for an early departure the next morning and decided to have our last night out on the 'front' with the 'druggies' and the 'yobs'. We returned at about 10:30pm to find that the apartment <u>had</u> been burgled. Tony, Dad and I had lost very little but John and Alex had been cleaned out. Clothes (yes even the dirty ones), passports, money and the keys to the hire car had all been taken. (Tony, Dad and I later reflected on the incident and were retrospectively affronted when I pointed out that our clothing had been rifled through and rejected whilst John's and Alex's had all been taken – obviously these were burglars with standards!) Luckily, the car was still there; it had a hidden button that had to be depressed for the ignition to work and it looked like they had failed to find it. The apartment had been entered through the rear galleria; the apartment behind ours was still unsold and had been left deliberately insecure by the builder. This practice, we later discovered, was normal. Rather than have intruders damage the doors and windows to an empty property, the builder preferred to leave the properties open so that intruders could quickly look around and see that there was nothing worth stealing. Unfortunately for us it also gave them access to the rear of our property. We rang the police to report the break-in but they didn't want to know – they only venture out if the thieves are still within sight. We were told to go to Torre de la Horadada the next day to get a denuncia (a document generated via the Spanish crime-reporting and complaints system). We spent the night taking it in turns to guard the hire car, as we were sure they would come back for it. I just hoped they didn't show up during my dad's turn because, despite being over 70 he is quite fit and had armed himself with an iron bar. Given the opportunity, he would certainly have done someone some serious damage. John and Alex wanted to go home and I couldn't blame them – I wanted to go myself. During my turn on guard duty, two guys, who looked more North African than Spanish, turned up for the car. They saw me and legged it, but I was sure that I recognised one of them as a cleaner, employed by the builders, who prepared completed apartments for the final handover. This made perfect sense as such people would be able to tip off their criminal friends as to which apartments were newly occupied, and thus yield rich pickings; all that new stuff ready for the taking. I followed the men from a distance and made sure that they knew I had 'clocked' them and had taken a note of their vehicle registration.

It was clear to all of us by now that we could not set off back as planned and that the van would not be returned on time. I had to ring the van hire company in the UK and extend the rental, which cost me another £250. We then contacted the car hire company, which provided a spare key quite quickly, and we then used the car to go to the police station. When we got there, the officer on duty pointed to a sign printed in English which indicated that we had to get an interpreter, so I then had to contact our friends from the property company who recommended a teenager called Darryl. Darryl was commissioned and, much to the dismay of the police, who must have thought they had seen the last of us, we returned to the police station to find the officer who had turned us away, speaking perfect English to an elderly couple. For some reason he didn't like the look of us and reverted to Spanish and dirty looks when it was our turn to be dealt with. Granted we did look a bit scruffy but then we *had* been stressed out, burgled, had had no sleep and John and Alex had nothing else to wear. Darryl told us that the attitude was not unusual and that he didn't know what the problem was but the officer was obviously not keen to deal with us. John and Alex had to itemise their losses, which took ages even with Darryl's assistance (iPod nano took rather a lot of explaining), and we asked for something that could be produced at the airport to cover the loss of their passports. The police instructed us to go to the British Consulate in Alicante for temporary passports. Finally, the denuncias were completed, Darryl was paid and we headed for Alicante.

After completing several circuits of the outskirts of Alicante we located the consulate and entered into another deli-counter style ticketing system. The temporary passports cost over £50 each and took a couple of hours to obtain – we needed passport-sized photographs for each of them and the consulate had no machine (if they had one they would make a fortune). Without further ado John and Alex were then deposited at the airport with no luggage. Extra costs were incurred changing the flights and we were told that we didn't actually need the temporary passports we had just spent ages getting because 'these things happen all the time' and the denuncia paperwork would have been sufficient. I bet the police had had a good laugh about that one.

Back at the apartment, Tony and Dad barricaded the back door with the 'hastily chosen from the gift voucher and very over-priced' washing machine and we set off back to Manchester. The whole burglary episode had been distressing from start to finish and John and Alex's test drive of the apartment was not the one we had planned. We had learned a lot about Spain but for all the wrong reasons. I felt sick.

To make matters worse Tony, Dad and I arrived at the Eurotunnel 12 hours after our ticket had expired and once that was sorted out we were then caught up in some French dispute which delayed our boarding even further. Eventually we got back to Manchester, and one very relieved hire company employee re-took possession of their truck.

You would have thought that now we would get a bit of a break but a few days later Tony's mum had a diabetic incident that necessitated the South Wales police breaking into her home and having her admitted to hospital. She had recently been diagnosed as being in the early stages of Alzheimer's disease, and this was affecting her ability to control her diabetic condition. She eventually recovered but would not accept any help from the social services for her insulin injections so 'hypos' became more frequent as her memory deteriorated. Unfortunately, that was only the start of the decline of our fortune (if it had not already begun with the attitudes of the property company, the Spanish police, and the Los Altos break in).

November 2005 –
Things Get Worse

In November 2005 something happened quite unexpectedly which was to change the course of everything. The winter weather in the UK had been getting steadily worse and Tony had been experiencing shortness of breath on the days when it was especially cold and damp. On one particular Saturday evening the noise from his chest was so loud that I suggested taking him into hospital to get it checked out. Tony refused as he was on weekend call-out and instead promised that he would go to his own doctor on the following Monday after work if it didn't get any better. Over the next couple of hours his breathing continued to deteriorate and, despite his protestations, I felt that I had no option but to call an ambulance. The paramedics who attended gave him oxygen and said he had to 'go in' and that I could not accompany him in the ambulance. I could follow in the car if I wished, but I had to forget it if they put the blue light on. I took this to mean that the blue light was looking like a distinct possibility and followed them in a state of utter terror. Thank God it never did come on. Tony was taken into accident and emergency and put onto a nebuliser to ease his breathing. By this time I was scared stiff and rang our friend Rod who came to sit with me whilst Tony was put through several tests to rule out a heart attack (his dad, of whom he is the spitting image, had had one big one and no second chances). After a chest X-ray and several other tests, the medical staff agreed on an interim diagnosis of COPD and we were left wondering what on earth that could be.

Tony was signed off work that night and was never to return but, thanks to the mindless 'push button, pull handle – don't think outside the box' procedures of local government (you can add to that recipe a big dollop of inefficiency and a 'we are going to bugger up your life just because we can' attitude), we were destined to spend too many precious months apart. COPD (Chronic Obstructive Pulmonary Disease) is a respiratory condition common in heavy smokers. We were told that it could ultimately prove to be terminal, and that the damage that was already done was permanent, but that if Tony gave up smoking, he could live longer and the condition may not get worse. He underwent rafts of tests, with his own doctor, the employer's doctor and a specialist. His prescriptions became longer and more expensive and we had to put aside a whole drawer just for his medication. My grandmother had had chronic emphysema so I had some idea of what lay ahead. Touchingly, the 'caring employer' was still in no rush to let him go despite the fact that he could not breathe without medication; perhaps they thought they could squeeze a few more months of work out of him before he suffocated?

Being the longer in service with the organisation, I had already handed in my resignation, as my notice period was longer than his. What did we do now? I considered the dreadful option of withdrawing my notice until things improved, but Tony has never been one to be defeated and insisted that we should continue as planned. The only thing that had changed in his perception was that they would now have to let him go on a medical basis and that his arrival in Spain would only be slightly delayed. The fact that they had not let him go voluntarily, with the accompanying reduction to his pension, was their undoing, and at least his illness had become apparent prior to him handing in his notice. This sort of positive thinking used to be quite alien to me, but I could see his point.

Mentally I had already geared myself up for getting out of the damned place so I was happy to proceed on that basis. I was fully capable of living in Spain for a few months on my own if that was what it took to continue with our plans and for Tony to be treated fairly. After all we had tried to be straight with them and they had rejected our attempts and responded with threats. With medical opinion now on his side I was hopeful that they would do the decent thing and let him go.

To maintain focus on our goal I designed a leaflet to advertise the Spanish apartment for rent and printed off enough to send out with our Christmas cards. At the end of December I received a letter informing me that the villa was ready and I left my employment. I had been so disillusioned with the place that I just wanted to go quietly with no fuss and had endeavoured to keep my plans to myself as far as possible. Disappointingly, my line manager saw fit to spoil my low-key departure by betraying professional confidences and leaving the rest to the gossips. He was advertising my post before I had even officially departed and my resignation, which I had submitted in strictest confidence directly to the Inhuman Resources Department, had become common knowledge within 48 hours of them receiving it. God forbid if anyone had something cringingly personal to confide. Anyway, to this day, and no matter how bad things became in the interim, I have never regretted turning my back on that place.

January 2006 –
Our Year? No Chance!

Tony reckoned that 2006 was going to be 'our year', and on January 13th I left Manchester with Peanut (my hamster) and the last of my personal belongings in my dad's old Ford Escort estate. Peanut didn't need a pet passport because he was smaller than a ferret (I had checked this out with DEFRA), but to be on the safe side we covered his cage up with a coat and failed to declare him to Customs on the way out. The Manchester flat had been temporarily taken off the market because Tony still needed somewhere to live and the market was as dead as a Dodo anyway. This was additional expense I had not expected to have to cover, but we were determined to carry on and make things work out. I was to live in the Spanish apartment and get it ready for rental, whilst moving things into the villa for our own use once I obtained the keys. We already had bookings coming in (I was using a trusted ex-colleague as my UK booking agent) and we were feeling confident that we could make the whole thing work. Tony was with me for the first week and then he had to go back for however long it took for his sickness to be sorted out (at this stage he was still undergoing tests to determine the severity of his COPD). He was certainly in no fit state to be moving boxes or furniture but it was good to have his company and there were things he could help me with. The first task was to buy a Spanish registered car and to get rid of the Escort. No caution was being applied at this stage, as no thoughts of failure were in our heads, and I really needed to get driving 'on the wrong side' before I lost my confidence.

I had been intending to buy a small van just in case I went ahead with a notion of setting up a cleaning business for holiday homes. We went around several car dealers and tried to find a car or van from one who would take the right-hand drive vehicle in part exchange. Unfortunately for us the correct vehicle was never with the right dealer, and in the end I got fed up and bought a tiny bright green Hyundai Atos from a Spanish dealer and sold my dad's Escort to a Brit in the car park of the local McDonald's (as you do). We had settled on the Atos simply because there are so many of them on the roads in Spain we knew we would have no trouble getting it fixed, trading it in or selling it privately if any of those needs arose. They are also remarkably economical to run. As is usual practice in Spain the dealer wanted payment in cash and, even though it was only a modest amount, the bank said the money would have to be ordered and I would have to return to collect it the next day. The next day it happened to be raining which, in turn, resulted in a power failure at the bank. When I turned up for my cash, I was told, "It is raining, we are not doing money today, please go somewhere else." Where? We literally had to wait for it to stop raining before we could have the car. The car dealer, being Spanish, did not seem to think this was strange. In fact, the only time he showed much emotion was as we left and the door to his office came off in Tony's hands; the dealer rolled his eyes, sighed, took his door back from Tony, and leaned it against his office wall before indicating that he would see us when the rain ceased.

Many British people prefer to use the British dealers in Spain, but I have to say that our Spanish dealer was very helpful and he even organised my insurance with Linea Direct (the Spanish equivalent of Direct Line). The policy charge was very reasonable and to my surprise covered any driver over the age of 26 and included breakdown cover. The documentation I had to produce in order to be able to buy the car included my NIE, a copy of the deeds to my apartment, and a copy of my passport. A certificate of 'No Claims' from my UK insurance company was required to obtain the insurance policy. The documents in my name came through six weeks later and I had to pick them up from the dealer; in the meantime, they issued me with a cover note. I was informed that all the vehicle documents had to be kept in the car (which is not something I would do back in the UK) and that I needed two yellow 'high visibility' jackets, two warning triangles, spare bulbs and a spare pair of specs or contact lenses if my vision needed correcting.

I was to get the keys to the villa a couple of days later so I spent the intervening time practising driving. For some reason, despite having driven in the UK for years, I turned into a female version of Frank Spencer once I got behind the wheel in Spain. This coupled with the fact that I felt pressurised by the natural impatience of Spanish drivers, led to some embarrassing moments but luckily none came to the notice of the police or caused any accidents. Be warned, Spanish roads have only had roundabouts on them for about ten years – older drivers have no idea how to use them and the younger ones, with their aversion to using their indicators, are not much better. The fatality rate on Spanish roads is one of the highest in Europe and for a race that is so laidback about life in general they become curiously manic when driving. No matter how fast you go it will not be fast enough. It took a couple of weeks of regular outings for me to begin to feel that driving on the right was natural and I now find it easier than I did at home. This may be partially due to the fact that the roads in this part of Spain are significantly quieter than those around Manchester. I am glad that I took up the gauntlet and started driving here as soon as I could because far too many people (especially women) lose their independence and end up far more isolated than they ought to be. This can only make the transition to the new life even more difficult, and believe me it is already difficult enough.

I also quickly enrolled at a local language school on a three-month conversational Spanish course. I was determined to start speaking 'the language' as soon as possible. I wanted to be able to hold my own at the town hall and the police station and the hospital and any other official venue I may have the misfortune to end up in. The course started off really well, albeit with the usual mundane topics, and I didn't miss any lessons for the first two months, but I then became distracted by issues with the villa and I lost my momentum. I never quite got it back, and my commitment to learning the language became less than satisfactory.

Eventually, the day came for us to take possession of the villa. We had been disappointed to find out that Pauline and Phil had been unable to sell their finca in the mountains and had therefore pulled out of buying in Los Montesinos and so would not be our neighbours after all. The property agent was to prove to be even more diabolical in their 'hand-over' service to us than they had been previously. I had had another altercation with them just before Christmas when a snotty woman (I think she would have described herself as 'assertive'), left a message on my answerphone in Manchester accusing me of failing to contact them about completion. As usual they had made an almighty cock-up and the arrangements were already in place. I received no apology – just some lame excuse about a breakdown in communication between their UK and Spanish offices. By now I just wanted to get the hand-over completed and to have nothing more to do with them as a customer. They sent an unpleasant old man round to deal with my 'moving in'. I was stuck with him for the best part of two days and he spent most of that time making it plain that he thought I was a pain in the arse. He also seemed to make great efforts to be as unhelpful as possible without actually doing anything I could legitimately complain about. At the end of the second day, following yet another 'faster than the speed of light' shopping trip, he left without even ensuring that I had received the keys – because he had another customer to 'look after' – God help them!

This time, in contrast to my experience with the builder of the apartment, the snagging list we had completed was not worth the paper it was written on. One way or another over the coming months I tended to the snags myself, as no one from the agent, or the builder, ever came to sort them out. The only issue I couldn't deal with was the lack of electricity in the kitchen. For this I had to go back to the builder's representative who was based in the show house. With kitchen equipment about to be delivered I went to report the lack of power – the rep. told me that Friday was not a good day to have an electrical problem and that it would be better if I had it on Monday! I was so stunned by the obvious lack of appreciation for my predicament and the degree of logic she displayed in her comment, that I did not argue, and dutifully reported back on the following Monday to confirm that no sockets had miraculously come to life over the weekend. The electrician eventually sauntered up the path on Wednesday evening and until then we ate out, and boiled the kettle on the floor in the hallway.

Very few people hold high opinions of property agents once the process has been *completed*, usually because it has not been *completed* to the satisfaction of the customer. The after-sales care is non-existent and the care in between would be unlikely to win any customer service awards. Once they have your deposit money, and you are contractually obliged to the builder, you are yesterday's news. My experience with the snagging list was all too common, and not confined to the agent I had dealt with. It is certainly not the norm for snags to be dealt with quickly and with no fuss. Knowing what I now know, I would recommend to anyone that they inspect the property thoroughly a couple of weeks before agreeing to complete. In this way they can insist that snags are corrected <u>before</u> the final payment is made and they will have time to inspect the remedial work before completing the purchase of the property with the notary.

Professional snagging companies do exist, so if individuals do not have the time to carry out the inspection themselves, they provide a convenient alternative for a reasonable fee and are well versed in the process. Once you have taken possession of your property it is standard practice for the builder to give you 15 days in which to report any further snags – they are then supposed to tend to those snags within 28 days. Many people then think that if they notice something after that period has expired, they can't do much about it. This would be quite unreasonable as clearly many properties do not get a decent test drive immediately as they are not permanently occupied. It is not a well-known or well-publicised fact that the builder is fully liable for the first 12 months for snags and faults unless they are down to misuse or wear and tear. It is clearly better though to get all snags dealt with in one go – you live and learn. If I had my time again, I would consider using a snagging company; caught up in the excitement and upheaval of a major move you fail to look at the correct things and hope that your agent is going to earn their money and do a good job for you. But in reality agents make a great performance of looking for cracked tiles and asking for the property to be cleaned but they don't dig too deeply or make a nuisance of themselves because they are ultimately in league with the builder and all they really want is your final payment so that they will get their commission. It is just business to them and you are part of the process.

With the nightmare agent now off our hands, the villa keys in our possession and bookings coming in for the apartment, I thought we could relax a bit and begin to establish a routine to our lives in Spain but there was one more trick up the sleeve of fate that would begin to sow the first small seeds of doubt in my mind.

To celebrate the completion of the villa purchase, Tony and I decided to have a couple of drinks in his favourite bar in Los Altos. We were into our second drink when I bent down to stroke a friend's dog and out of the corner of my eye saw Tony hit the tiled floor headfirst. He looked dead. I thought he had emulated his dad and had one big, no second chances, heart attack. He was out cold and froth was coming from the corner of his mouth. I patted his face and shouted his name and eventually his eyes opened. One of the other customers in the bar came over to help, the rest were shocked and stunned into inactivity and kept a polite British distance. Tony would not accept that he had passed out and was embarrassed to find himself on the floor. I was advised to get him checked out at the hospital. This was my first big reality check – I didn't know where the hospital was! Back home I would have known exactly what to do but here in Spain I felt totally lost. Tony refused to be taken anywhere and just said he wanted to go to bed. Reluctantly I complied with his wishes, but I was scared to death and burst into tears the moment I was alone. I spent a sleepless night constantly checking that he was still breathing – so much for the celebration. The next morning he seemed to be back to his usual self and said the only thing he could remember was coughing a lot before he came round on the floor of the bar. We took it steady for the next couple of days and made a dummy run to the local hospital so that I would know how to get there if there was a repeat performance, then Tony returned back to Manchester and left Peanut and I to sort things out. I was worried sick about Tony but people had paid me hard-earned money for their holidays so I had to make sure that I delivered them.

My first customers, Kim and Steve, were personal friends and they were due in the apartment around mid-March so I had about six weeks to get it ready and to move all our personal stuff up to the villa. I moved half a dozen boxes a day, got to know my immediate neighbours, practised my appalling Spanish on the local farmer who kept me supplied with citrus fruit, got plenty of driving practice, went to my Spanish classes and lost a fair bit of weight. I was beginning to enjoy myself; I felt free and I was busy. It looked like everything was, at last, starting to work out just fine. The villa was not in an organised state and did not yet feel like home but the apartment was looking good; the grilles were up and the safe keys had been obtained. I was sure my guests would be happy, secure and comfortable. Our own comfort would have to wait. Back home Tony had been checked out by his own doctor and was told that he had experienced a bout of 'cough syncope'. This is a condition that leads to a blackout when excessive coughing (caused by the COPD) brings about a sudden drop in blood pressure. It was something we were both going to have to be aware of as there was no knowing how often, or where, it would happen again.

March 2006 –
Welcome To Spain (Not) 2

Over the next few weeks I was happy enough. The urbanisation at Los Montesinos was still only sparsely inhabited and my nearest neighbours were several plots away. I had met a small number of people who all seemed pleasant, but I very much kept myself to myself and concentrated on what needed to be done. The few people I had met had seemed over-eager to tell me their life stories, sometimes in far too much detail, and I was reluctant to reciprocate until I knew them a bit better and had decided whether or not I wanted to be friends with them. As we had not yet been fully adopted by the town council our street lighting was not working, so the area became very dark at night and I rarely ventured far; preferring instead to batten down the hatches and read a good book (a Spanish neighbour later confided that he thought that he could tell which houses were occupied by Brits because "You all go in when it gets dark"). I felt quite safe but, with our Los Altos experience still fresh in my mind, one of the first things I had done when I moved into the villa was to get the pre-installed Securitas alarm system activated.

The Securitas engineer was a nice chap and I was surprised when he told me that some of the residents had had the Securitas system removed and an 'English' one put in. In my opinion the Securitas service is excellent. They monitor the system remotely and alert you when it is going off. They let you know if there has been a power failure, which is very useful if you are away and your freezer is full of things that will start to defrost; this happens quite a lot when you are still on 'builder's electricity'. The transmitter enables them to speak to you directly without a phone, and they speak excellent English. There is a panic button and a direct means of calling for the fire brigade or ambulance service (which made me feel better even though I hoped I would never have to use it). They also have coded ways of telling if you are in trouble even if someone is standing there holding a knife to your throat telling you what to say. Why would you have it taken out? The answer – money – it's nearly as expensive as it is in England. Well yes it is, but I think it is also a better service. I also think it is true to say that many people come to Spain expecting life here to be <u>much</u> cheaper than it is at home. It isn't, you just tend to spend your money on different things like running air conditioning instead of central heating. Out-of-date repeats of holiday home TV programmes quoting prices from years ago create a false impression of what is achievable and I would advise anyone to check current rates before making any financial plans and to try to discover the average running cost of a property before committing themselves to a purchase.

Mid-March arrived and so did Kim and Steve. The weather was changeable and I inexplicably became anxious about the success of their holiday. They are people who would not be fazed by a bit of drizzle but I really wanted my first customers to be able to go back and say it was great. Tony obtained permission from his line manager to leave the country whilst unfit for work and came back out for a short break. We tried to make the best of the uncomfortable situation at the villa; I was still living out of boxes, and the lack of organisation coupled with no telephone and no computer, was very frustrating. However, I was still feeling quite upbeat about the whole move. We took Kim and Steve out a couple of times and on their last evening Tony took them back to the airport whilst I cleaned the apartment. When he came back for me we decided to go for a Chinese meal in the Punta Prima area before going back to Los Montesinos. As we were leaving, my Spanish mobile rang – it was Securitas – the alarm at the villa was going off and they had called the police. We got back to the villa as quickly as possible, and at first it looked like a false alarm. The police were not there and the villa appeared to be still secure. By the time we got to the front door however, we could see that some maniac had been hacking at it with a sharp tool. There were splinters of wood everywhere, chunks out of the lovely door and the granite step was chipped. Inside I deactivated the alarm. Whoever it was had not gained entry, but the episode was enough to burst my bubble. Our nearest Spanish neighbours, a citrus farmer and his wife, came over and explained that they had heard banging, and had shouted across and scared off whoever it was. The police had been and gone. The alarm company called me back to see if everything was all right and they said they would send the police back. After our previous experience at Torre de la Horadada I was not enthusiastic about this but they came anyway – in droves – it was like a Guardia Civil and Policia Local social event in our garden. They were a complete contrast to the police in Torre, very pleasant and very laidback about the whole thing. "No entrada", and much shrugging of shoulders summed the situation up. They took a digital photograph of our battered front door, spoke to the farmer and left. The farmer's wife offered me a drink to make me 'muy tranquillo' and Tony pointed out that the alarm and the door had done their jobs and that we were lucky to have such wonderful neighbours.

His argument was compelling but inside I had flipped and was beginning to plan my escape back to crime-ridden Manchester where I knew the ropes.

A couple of days later, as Tony packed to go home, I discovered that Peanut had died in the night. He was very precious to me and had been my only company on the long, lonely nights. His death was the final straw and I snapped. What had we done to deserve all this? We weren't scrounging off anyone, we had never done anyone any harm, and we were taking a massive gamble to live simpler, calmer lives – why couldn't we just have a break, rather than a flaming break-in?

We buried Peanut under a cactus plant that Kim and Steve had bought us. I rang my dad and cried down the phone (about Peanut but not the attempted break in – I hadn't told him about that or he would probably have done some caveman thing and come to cart me back off home). I then went down to the local Internet café and booked a ticket for the same flight home that Tony was on. If Peanut hadn't died I would have had to have stayed, but now I couldn't see the point. It was ten days to my next guest's arrival, and I was going to spend seven of them in lovely, cold and rainy Manchester. I went down the street to tell my nearest neighbour Janet (whom I had met at a community meeting about the lack of telephones) that I was going home for a few days. She agreed to keep an eye on the place for me. I remember saying I didn't really care any more if the villa got cleaned out because that would just mean I had less stuff to move back to Manchester. In fact, I considered leaving the door wide open to help the process along (at least then there would be less damage done).

My seven days at home were a mistake. I should have stayed in Spain and toughed it out. My mind was in turmoil and Tony must have wondered where this unhinged manic-depressive had suddenly appeared from, because I certainly wasn't the woman he was used to living with. I hardly left the flat and spent a great deal of time in bed hoping that the world would just sod off out of my life. Unsurprisingly my dad made 'pack it in and come home' noises (and he didn't know the half of it) and he, and my brother, Rob, were so supportive that I ended up feeling guilty on top of everything else. Before I left, my dad, seeing an opportunity to get me back on British soil, and not being one to let such an opportunity pass, offered to keep the flat in Manchester running for a while until we were sure that we were going to stay put in Spain. I'm sure he had his fingers crossed that I would come to my senses and get myself back where I belonged. It was a lifeline that I was lucky to be thrown and one I was not going to refuse. To hell with pride, I just wanted a sure-fire means of escape! It was agreed that the flat was not going back onto the market and when the seven days were up Tony enthusiastically packed me back off to Spain to pull myself together.

April 2006 –
Back In Spain

It took me a few days to adjust to being back in the villa, and I didn't sleep much the first night on my own following the assault on the front door. Colin, the guy who fitted the grilles at the apartment after our first 'welcome to Spain', was commissioned to put a metal gate over the front door and window locks on all the windows (even though these already had grilles fitted). Plus I had the alarm. I was effectively sealed in – the place was a cross between Strangeways and Fort Knox. I had never had this level of security back in Manchester and was beginning to feel like a prisoner in my new 'home'.

I gave myself a good talking-to about not giving up and I knew that I had to stay anyway to run the apartment. I needed to find an outlet; something to keep my mind occupied. A couple of weeks later I began writing. I was angry at the portrayal of the whole process as being easy. I was sick of hearing of scams and swindles that no one had cared to warn me about, but which apparently went on 'all the time'. I was incensed that good people had taken chances with their lives and their life savings and that too many of them were having the same unpleasant experiences. For once in my life I had things to say that might be of benefit to someone else. So I got started. Luckily, I found it easier to express myself when I was feeling particularly bad, so writing became an outlet for my frustrations and anxiety and, in a way, it made me feel much better. Occasionally I would look back at what I had written and think that I sounded like a miserable cow – but then at that particular moment in time I probably *was* a miserable cow.

As I was still without the comforts of any technology, I began to add to the general mess at the villa with bits of paper bearing my thoughts on topics that needed to be covered. I desperately missed having a computer or a telephone.

During the next few weeks I had several guests at the apartment, which kept me busy and made time pass much more quickly. At such times my spirits lifted and I began to feel more confident about what I was doing. I spent my spare time trying to make the villa more homely, though deep down I felt I was only kidding myself because I had already fallen out of love with it. My neighbours, in the main, were lovely, and I couldn't fault Los Montesinos but still I couldn't quite settle down. I became obsessed with locking the front door. If I went onto the roof terrace or even around the back of the villa I felt the need to lock up. (In the following months I was to miss several telephone calls because I couldn't get back in quickly enough to answer them.)

It was around this time that I had balustrades fitted onto the veranda for a bit more privacy when sitting outside and had the weed-infested soil gravelled over as a temporary measure, pending the decision as to whether or not we were going to have a swimming pool. The farmer came over and gave the builders tips on spreading gravel and told me I was making a big mistake for not having a membrane put down. He was right but it was significantly cheaper not to have it. The guys who had installed my air-conditioning had recommended the builders to me and they did a good job. Prior to me setting them on, I had been pestered by a Ukrainian called Vlad who had a team working in the area. His quotes were certainly much cheaper, but after the break-in attempt I was nervous of dealing with anyone with whom I could not fully communicate and I wanted to deal with legal workers whom I could contact if I was not satisfied with their workmanship.

I mentioned the big differences in the quotes to my builder and he said that he could not compete with such low prices. He said that the only way he could imagine someone making a profit like that was if they were coming by their materials in a less than honest fashion. I took this to mean that the 'low quoters' were most probably nicking their materials from building sites and simply charging for the labour.

At this stage my thoughts were never far away from a full return to Manchester and I just wanted the villa to look smart for resale if that is what I chose to do. The argument against this was that there were several villas of the same style still up for sale through the show house, so the prospect of a quick sale was remote. My philosophy had to change for me to be able to survive.

Holiday bookings at the apartment meant that there was no chance of me going back to Manchester for a visit before July, when there were a couple of weeks free, so I had to knuckle down and get on with it. If I felt *really* bad I occasionally confided in Janet, but I was aware that in doing so I might set her off and drag her down with me so usually I just bottled it up. I really didn't like talking to anyone on the subject apart from Tony because my emotions were seriously inconsistent and contradictory. Given the chance I could change attitude in mid-sentence.

Janet did know what I was going through, as she had been in Spain about six months longer than I had and had already had more than one mental meltdown. We were both having similar trouble. Most of it centred on a lack of things to do. The tedium was getting to us. Both of us had had busy jobs back home and been used to not having enough time in the day to do everything that needed doing. The almost 'dead stop' life in Spain was a massive, and inexplicably unpleasant, shock to the system. Whilst I was working I had always imagined that it would be great to have lots of spare time, but the reality of it wasn't shaping up that way.

To my dismay I started to kill time watching daytime TV. I had never been a big TV watcher, always preferring to read, but now I had enough time to do both and I knew it wasn't achieving anything. I had ceased to improve on my spoken Spanish, I wasn't integrating and overall I wasn't very happy. (I am fairly sure it was George Bernard Shaw who said 'A perpetual holiday is a good working definition of Hell'. Well, I don't know what led him to that conclusion, but it sure sums up the way I was feeling.) Luckily, towards the middle of April two things happened to save me from complete insanity. The phone was connected – yeeehaaaa, and I bought a computer – double yeeehaaaa. I was in touch with the outside world once more, I could surf the net and talk to Tony, Dad, and Rob without going bankrupt (I had been using my mobile and it was very expensive). Also, I could finally get rid of all of those bits of paper I was keeping notes on. Hallelujah, thank you God!

It may seem like a small thing, but to me it was fantastic. I spent all the first afternoon calling people with my new number and saying "I'm connected!"; it also made me feel safer and less cut off from my loved ones. My mood improved and my spirit for the venture returned.

Home Improvements

I have noticed that after people have taken possession of a brand new foreign property, especially one with a little outside space, many immediately begin to distract themselves from the reality of the move by busying themselves with 'personalising' the place, instead of taking their time and making slow improvements after shopping around, and having a good old nosey at what other people have had done.

The speed at which they launch themselves into these projects can be frightening. They take on workmen who simply turn up at the gate touting for jobs or someone they have heard about in a bar. Swimming pools, patios, balustrades, gazebos and barbecues spring up at great cost and with alarming speed. The workmen then quickly disappear and are un-contactable when cracks and leaks begin to appear. Apart from the financial implications, bad workmanship can make a property look worse rather than better and can certainly affect the owner's ability to resell if unfortunate incidents or personal crises force a rapid return to the UK.

Owing to the uncertainty of our (especially Tony's) circumstances and my (hopefully temporary) mental instability, we were more cautious than most when it came to getting work done. I felt that if I did not settle and wanted to move back home then the property would be more attractive to a prospective purchaser as a 'blank canvas' and we would certainly be able to put a competitive price on it having not spent anything extra on it ourselves.

As neighbours' pools filled around us, we held onto our cash and planned a very slow improvement to the garden area. In the meantime, I took on the highly recommended and properly registered builder to carry out my balustrade job so that I could assess his work, see if he was reliable and, more importantly for me, decide whether I got on well with him and would trust him in the house if I had to nip out. One lady I spoke to arrived home to find one of her Russian 'builders' asleep in her bed and the other drinking her husband's beer whilst watching TV with his feet up on the coffee table. She was unable to communicate with them as an intermediary had set them on and she was afraid to attempt to dismiss them.

My builder told me of an even more frightening incident in which, during the conversion of an under-build (cellar) into a games room and bar, some eastern European builders had removed the footings to the front of a house. Apparently, to the novice in building matters, it looked like they had done a good job and the man of the house was eager to show off this particular room to all who visited. Luckily he showed it to a man he had invited round to give him a quote for a pool. The pool man looked horrified and said there was no way he, or anyone else, was going to be building a pool on this property as, if a hole was dug out in the area available, the front of the house was now so weak that it was likely to slide off into it. To date this particular house has been declared structurally unsound after large cracks began to appear in the front wall. Needless to say, the 'builders' have vanished.

Even though our approach cost us slightly more we did benefit from having jobs done well first time. Our builder and his mate turned out to be marvellous and we planned to call them back to do our pool and patio if we decided to stay. Too many people we know have been left with uneven paving and unfinished work; their properties left looking more like building sites than homes. The manager of one pool company threatened to break the legs of a resident's family members after the man withheld the final payment in a dispute over a cracked drain. Naturally he paid up, and then had to have the work corrected by someone else. The extra costs incurred for remedial work and 'making good' too frequently transform a cheap job into a stressful false economy, and registered tradesmen are naturally reluctant to spend time and effort putting right someone else's poor workmanship when they were not employed to do the job from scratch.

We encountered similar issues with the installation of our air conditioning. I drove Tony mad looking at different units and scrutinising the advertisements for air conditioning installers printed in the local papers – especially those that said 'Panasonic' in them (I have to admit to having a weakness for this brand as nothing built by Panasonic has ever let me down – I threw my 1970s music centre away in 2001 because the bloody thing just would not die and it was so big it was making me a laughing stock). One thing that concerned me though was that hardly any of them just did air conditioning; they did TV installation and 'small electrical work' and plumbing; airport pick-ups and pet sitting and building work, 'no job too small'. These ads had an air of desperation about them and failed to convey any sort of skill. In the end I found one company who just did air con' even though there was no mention of Panasonic. I rang and was immediately told "We are not cheap!" This company only dealt with a high quality brand called Daikin. I had never seen the brand in any of the shops. I met the installer and was impressed with his product knowledge and his honest admission that the job would be expensive. I became the proud owner of a couple of thousand euros worth of Daikin 'hot and cold' air conditioning. The company did such a great job on the apartment that I had them back to do the villa. Daikin air conditioning is efficient, it is economical, and it is quiet and very reliable. I can recommend it. As far as we were concerned, it was money well spent; the job was neat, the fitters were skilled and prompt and I got a guarantee. If asked by neighbours I am quick to praise this system and the company I obtained it from – I then have to help them to a chair to get over the price. They tell me they got their units from the local hypermarket for only a couple of hundred euros each and that they fitted them themselves – they have big holes in the sides of their properties to prove it. Months later they will invariably report that their units are noisy or not working properly, they drip condensation into the room and the electricity bill has just arrived and the air conditioning is proving to be so expensive to run that they daren't have it on. At the end of the summer months I compared an electricity bill with that of a neighbour and was shocked to see that mine was €150 less for the same two-month period. If the disparity continued I could reasonably expect to have paid around €1000 less than my neighbours during a 12-month period. In the space of only three years the system would pay for itself as I saved on my bills. I have it on all night without worrying and I don't need a separate heating system for the winter. What more can I say except that, occasionally, you *do* get what you pay for!

Before carrying out any external alterations it is advisable to check whether the work involved requires any permission or licence from the town hall. Too many conflicting stories are told in the local bars for any of the information gleaned to be of much use. I had been told by several people that wooden and aluminium structures that were merely bolted down were regarded as 'temporary' and therefore did not require any permission, but a builder with several years' experience working on the Costa Blanca told me that *everything* except painting was regulated. I was also advised that if I sought a licence for all structures and kept the bills from the town hall that I would be able to deduct such charges from any capital gains tax when I came to sell. This was sufficient for me to err on the side of caution, even though I knew that plenty of people had 'got away with' the erection of wooden and aluminium structures. In the built-up and heavily populated areas of the Costa Blanca it is relatively easy to escape detection if you are tempted to carry out unauthorised building work, but in a small town like Los Montesinos this is not the case. The Policia Local act as agents for the town hall and patrol regularly in search of illegal extensions to patio tiling and other horrendous crimes such as having a shed large enough to live in. They are quick to challenge builders for the appropriate paperwork showing that the correct tax has been paid, and they have the power to order the work to stop if such paperwork cannot be produced.

If you enter a system which is not your own, you have to make an effort to understand what is required of you within that system before you can really accomplish whatever it was that was driving you in the first place. If you don't then you will find obstacles arise at every stage and this only adds to your frustration. Many people just cannot be bothered to get the correct documents together for work done to their properties, either to avoid paying the taxes or because they don't want to pay a translator and don't feel confident to deal with whatever it is themselves. This is fine if you 'get away with it', but you really can't complain if you get caught and fined. Others end up with properties that are awash with 'temporary structures' and a mishmash of ideas that don't complement one another.

When you first arrive, especially if you have bought a brand new property, you will inevitably be pestered by the local know-all who will be eager to 'help' you get discounts on work done on your property. The main culprit on our urbanisation was known as 'Mr Backhander'. He had his fingers in most pies – mobile phones, airport runs, key holding, cleaning and building work. At the first approach he would be very nice and he would catch newcomers off-guard. There are many dissatisfied customers of his now dotted around the estate but he is so hard-nosed he never stops. He has now branched out into driving lessons, karaoke, and catering. Maybe it is where many of us have gone wrong as there is no doubt that he has an instinct for survival, even if it means he ends up unpopular and with few genuine friends.

I firmly believe now that any 'improvements' made to your property should be done for your own use and enjoyment and not because they will add value to your property. In today's market, where the rock-bottom price is king, buyers will not be interested in how much was spent bringing your property up to the standard it is in. If your pool, glass curtains, or garden design is what attracted potential purchasers to view your property rather than another, then you have to regard it as a bonus, but don't expect to even get your money back, never mind make a profit. Before having any work done consider whether you are going to enjoy your money's worth of fun or use out of it before you move on. If the answer is no, and it is not essential, then take my advice and don't bother.

Getting It Into Perspective

It seems an obvious thing to say, but relocating abroad requires you to make serious adjustments to your life and these take time no matter how well you have planned your move. There is always going to be an element of risk in being so far away from home, where things are not the same as you are used to. Over time, we evolve lifestyles which are comfortable and with which we are able to cope. This means life will be fine so long as nothing much changes. Coping with many changes, country, job, language, system, and friends is no small thing so it should not come as any surprise that just when you need them most you are likely to have the least amount of confidence or resilience. It seems to me that rootless people are the ones who cope the best simply because for them change is what they are used to.

A few people will profess to have settled into their new lifestyle within minutes of unpacking, but for many the transition can be quite painful no matter how prepared and committed they think they are. If, like us, you choose a country where you are significantly less than fluent in the local language then there will be days when your own frustration with yourself drives you crazy. Also, if only one of you speaks any of the language, that individual can become sick and tired of speaking for the other. We all take communication so much for granted that when simple conversation becomes an effort you can become quite depressed. There were several occasions when I felt like I'd completely lost the plot. In fact I felt that I had never really had a plot, I had forgotten why I wanted to be here. Self-criticism would take over and I would go into a downward spiral of self-recrimination and gut-churning homesickness. Having relocated within the UK twice before, completely on my own, this left me stunned. I had envisaged some problems, but homesickness had never been a consideration. I didn't believe it would ever be something I would, or could, suffer from.

'Down' times such as these can consume you completely if you don't have enough to do during your day to keep yourself distracted. You then become incapable of making rational decisions. Panic moves at such times are responsible for people losing substantial sums of money in their attempts to restore something resembling the normality of their 'old' lives. They resell at a loss just to get out. I was lucky enough to have made friends with a number of people who had been in Spain for several years and who counselled me against panic remarketing, but there were occasions when I was sufficiently miserable not to care whether it was the sensible thing to do or not. In my more lucid moments I knew they were right. I also knew that my 'old' life was no longer there and that there were aspects of it that I did not want restoring no matter how bad things got. However, just after the attempted break-in at the villa, I did panic and sent a text to Pauline at the property company to say that I had had enough and was going to sell both properties. I asked her to recommend someone who could sell property really quickly. I was made to calm down and think straight. Not everyone is as lucky as I am though, and I know of at least three couples who could not stick with their plans because they were not able to adjust and could not get out fast enough. Their dreams quickly became very expensive errors. One pair bought an apartment for £90000 and sold it less than six months later for only £60000 – in that time the woman had been mugged, their apartment had been burgled three times and they were thoroughly sick of the place. People will say that the same could have happened back home but I had *never* been burgled in Manchester and I *was* burgled *twice* within eight months in Spain. You can't argue with the facts, and such experiences are bound to colour your judgement.

In order to retain some sense of control over the situation, you have to take a step back from it so that in your determination to sort out the mess you think you have created, you manage not to get yourself more deeply into trouble. At times like these you are vulnerable so it is best to keep away from the bar-room experts who always know someone who will 'help you out'; such 'Good Samaritans' are rarely what they seem and are more likely to be sharks who survive from other people's misfortune. For me it was preferable to simply prop the situation up and leave it well alone until my head cleared. Tinkering with it whilst you are low is more likely to just make things worse. Most scenarios should not be catastrophic but they will take time to unravel. Remind yourself that your property should be a long-term investment, and that so long as you conduct yourself sensibly you should lose nothing except your immediate sanity.

Still, it is difficult to express the feeling of despair that homesickness causes. It is all- encompassing and quite debilitating and it certainly hit me in large waves periodically between March and June 2006. During such times I would be unable to eat properly, I could not think positively and was terrible company. It wasn't a permanent state of mind but it caught me out at the most unexpected times, and was often triggered by a comment or action from someone else. I have never before known misery like it and

I was perfectly willing to share my unhappiness with Tony, even over the phone. I resented the fact that he was still living happily in Manchester and accused him of treating me like his own personal 'Forward Reconnaissance Unit'. This was totally unfair of me, and there was nothing Tony could do to change the speed of the process in which he was caught up with the 'caring employer', but he took the brunt of my frustration because I did not really feel able to talk to anyone else; I didn't want to worry my dad and I didn't want to become a source of either anxiety or entertainment for old friends and colleagues, so I only contacted them on the days when I felt positive.

I think what you miss most of all is the feeling of being in control and truly belonging somewhere; somewhere that is genuinely 'home'. Despite the wonderful views of the mountains and salt lakes, the marvellous climate and hospitable locals, you can be hit head-on by the realisation that you don't yet really belong here, and you wonder whether you ever will. When you are feeling low, it can be difficult to believe that it will get better, but that level of comfort takes time to develop and it is unreasonable to expect the safe and cosy feelings of home to be immediately transferable. You have to put the effort in to get them back. You have to become familiar with your surroundings, make new friends and get to know the system. These things don't happen overnight. There was once an advert on TV that said 'normal is great when you get it back'. I had reached a stage where I no longer knew what 'normal' was but one way or the other I knew I had to somehow reinstate it.

For me, the worst time of day between March and June was the moment I opened my eyes, saw the Securitas alarm box winking at me from the bedroom wall, and realised that *yes*, I was still in Spain and that *no*, it was not just an hilariously bad dream. My heart and stomach would go through sickening manoeuvres, my brain would kick in and I would start to worry about money and begin to re-evaluate my escape plots to get back to Manchester to get a 'proper' job. I found the best solution to this was to get out of bed and go for a walk straight away. If I continued to lie in bed for any length of time my mental discomfort would increase, but if I took a bit of exercise I would soon start to relax and feel good again and my anxiety would quickly dissipate. I would look around and appreciate my surroundings and I would feel grateful for my good fortune in having the opportunity to actually do something that many others just dream of doing.

When Tony was with me I felt much better but he was totally bewildered by my inconsistency. I couldn't blame him; it must be hard to be with someone who is plagued with misery in what should be happy times, but he failed to say the right things. At times the only thing I wanted to hear from him was that if I really didn't want to stay we could sell up and go home. He never indicated this as an option and so, in the early stages of the transition, I feared for our relationship if I couldn't get my head together once and for all. More than ever, I felt that the onus was entirely on me for this thing to work – and I was no longer convinced that it would, or that I really wanted it to.

There is no doubt that it is essential to keep the whole thing in proportion and perspective. You must do something constructive to improve your situation. Try not to dwell on the negative; wait, distract yourself with something useful, and resist the temptation to drown your sorrows in alcohol. Above all, do not sit back and ignore your predicament. It will not just go away all by itself.

Beware Of Sharks In The Property Pond

My 'escape back to Manchester' plots developed into a growing obsession with estate agents and solicitors. I collected their business cards and scrutinised their web sites for clues as to whether they were rip-off merchants or decent, honest and trustworthy operators.

If anyone mentioned selling a property I would unashamedly grill them for all the details (in my previous life I would never have dreamed of asking such personal questions). Which agent were they using and why, how much commission was the agent charging and most importantly would they recommend them? Quite often, the reply would be that the agent had sold the property with very little enthusiasm, was very expensive and that the seller would not want to deal with them again. This was not what I wanted to hear. Some of the better known 'international' companies will charge up to 18% to sell a villa and they will want the deeds to your house, power of attorney, a sole selling agreement, two sets of keys and an undertaking that the property will not be occupied whilst it is on their books (and I used to think UK estate agents were bad!). As far as I'm concerned a commission charge of 18% is a total piss-take and the conditions attached are too specific. Anyway they all ended up on my 'rip-off merchants' list.

Conversely, I was given the number of "A lovely bloke who only charges a flat rate fee of €5000", but after my now expert grilling, it transpired that the vendor had had her property on the market for over two years and had not had one single viewer! Not the best advert for a quick sale, especially if you are desperate to leave.

A neighbour gave me the number of "A lifelong family friend and all round good egg" who sold properties quicker than you could say 'Jack Robinson' and "only charges around €15000". Still, at the time, that was around £10000 but I got my hopes up. I took a card, scrutinised the website and then realised that the neighbour was unlikely to slag off his mate. Another well-meaning person then advised me that the mate was probably paying commission to the neighbour and, without any further justification, I began to smell a big rat. My suspicions were totally unjustified and were based on an offhand comment from someone I hardly knew. This level of paranoia makes committing to one agent very difficult, to such an extent that one acquaintance had her property for sale with 15 different companies – and she was still ripped off in a big way by a private purchaser who persuaded her to do a property swap.

Such wide variations in fees, combined with high levels of scaremongering and too much conflicting advice could have you reaching for the gin in no time at all. The best you can do is to decide what outcome is correct for you in your circumstances and choose the agent you feel is best fitted to deliver that specific result. There will be too many people ready to tell you that your agent is a crook and that you have made a bad decision. Ask yourself do you know this person any better than you know the agent? There are plenty of bar-room know-alls out there. Just do your own homework, pick a reputable company and don't take risks that you would not take at home (there was no way I was handing my deeds over to anyone except my solicitor).

Unfortunately, the level of greed within the property market is such that those expats who wish to return home and are desperate to do so inevitably become sitting ducks for the sharks swimming in the property pond and, contrary to popular belief, it is usually Brits ripping off other Brits. What is more frustrating is that there is a culture of 'name your own price' in Spain rather than a true market valuation. This can leave you bewildered as to what price to ask in order to get your property to sell without giving it away. The agent will add their fee on to the price you want to achieve and advertise it accordingly. The buyer therefore technically pays the agent's add-on fee, but it can often have the effect of over-pricing the property so that no buyer would be interested. This is why many people try to save money by putting up their own ´For Sale´ boards and attempt to handle the matter privately. It is not an option I personally thought I would favour, but with agents' fees generally varying between €5000 and €30000 it pays to do some serious research before appointing an agent (after all, a fee of £20000 in the UK would be charged for the sale of a property in the region of £1 million, and I, for one, am a long way off that price bracket). If you then factor in the fees and taxes you paid when you purchased and then knock off any capital gains (currently 18% for both residents and non-residents) that you will pay on any 'profit', it soon becomes clear that it can be difficult to break even if you have to resell within the first couple of years. The Spanish practice of making a proportion of the payment in cash and under-valuing the property on the deeds, can actually put you in a false profit situation on resale so that you could end up paying capital gains even when you haven't gained! This practice is difficult to avoid, as it is countenanced right up to notary level. There is no doubt that the practice is initially of benefit to the buyer (who only pays purchase tax on the value shown on the deeds), and it is of even greater benefit to the builder who saves tax on each property sold. But as the buyer is likely to eventually become a seller, ultimately the only real beneficiary is the builder.

In the excitement of relocation, the majority of us plan well for the move and fail to consider the possibility that it will not work out. We therefore have no contingency plan for when things start to go awry. I think that every proposed purchase of foreign property should come with the warning that 'short-term changes of mind can seriously damage your wealth'.

It is my belief that in this area of the Costa Blanca there is no quick profit to be made on property any more unless you operate on a less than scrupulous level, or have the time, money, and nerve to take on the development of a run-down property. Estate agents are expensive and taxes are high, so it is important to be clear of your reasons for buying before you commit yourself. Reselling in an area that is still under construction is especially difficult because the likes of you and I cannot compete with the builders' prices and perks, particularly if they still have many units to sell. If sheer profit is the driving force behind your purchase (ours wasn't) then be prepared to hold on to the property for a few years before trying to resell. Better still, look somewhere else for a newer 'emerging market'.

The Advantages Of Resale Properties

For the buyer there are many advantages to the resale property market of which the companies dealing in 'new builds' don't inform you. Consequently, you find out far too late and end up kicking yourself. For a start you can see the actual property and what surrounds it, not just a two-dimensional plan and an artist's impression. The local infrastructure will already be established and issues with local services and disputes with developers *should* be a thing of the past. Access roads, bus services, and street lighting will be in place and finished off and you can see how far it is to the local shops. Many a new development comes with the promise of a commercial centre or a bus route only for neither of them ever to materialise.

Not far from Los Montesinos is a development known locally as the 'forgotten urbanisation'. Two town councils were in dispute over which of them was responsible for it, and whilst this dispute continued, the residents had no facilities and nowhere to send their children to school. On another development, the residents of a large block of new apartments in the Pilar de la Horadada area found themselves with no water when the builders pulled off site and disconnected the 'builder's water' prior to the connection of the official paid-for supply. Without habitation certificates the residents were stuck, the place began to stink and no one could sell up because no right-minded individual would have touched the place with a bargepole. There is no doubt that the majority of these situations eventually get sorted out but it can take a very long time – and by that I mean *years*.

One couple we know were unfortunate enough to buy from a builder who had failed to wait for the correct permissions to be issued for the third phase of his development, having assumed that because phases one and two had been approved then so would phase three. He just got cracking and built and sold the houses. His assumption was ill-founded however, and the permissions did not materialise, with the result that this unfortunate couple, along with a number of others, ended up owning properties that they were not allowed to inhabit. In fact even after they had paid for their property they still did not officially have a key and thus were not able to retrieve the furniture that had been supplied as part of the deal. So much trust is put in the system, and many good people are taken advantage of. This couple had taken proper legal advice, bought through a large well-established agent, and followed all the correct procedures, only to be badly let down by those with whom they were dealing. The council in the area concerned is slowly negotiating with the builder to rectify the problem but three years have passed and, in the meantime, this couple can neither live in, nor sell, a property they have paid for. To make matters worse they had already sold up in the UK and now have to rent in Spain even though they own a vacant property. Clearly this sort of stress is not what you intend to inflict upon yourself when making a major investment in a new property in a foreign land.

With a resale property, you can see how populated an urbanisation really is and how well it has been maintained. Many properties that fall within the 'holiday home' category stand empty for months on end; their gardens are overgrown and their ironwork is covered with a thick layer of dust. In contrast, the well-kept properties of the permanent residents stick out like sore thumbs. Another distinct advantage is that telephone connections may well be already established; waiting to be connected is one of the frustrations of a new Spanish property – that is if they intend to connect you at all. One lady I met at Spanish classes had been waiting for over three years and had spent a fortune on mobile phone top ups in the meantime; another was connected within six weeks. It really is a lottery. Telefonica (the Spanish equivalent of BT) informed me quite bluntly when I rang to enquire about a line in the villa that they would not be connecting me because it was too much trouble; our development was too isolated and was simply not worth the trouble it would put them to. They told other residents that we would have to wait for two to three years as they had run out of numbers. We eventually got together and were connected en masse by a smaller company: a reasonably reliable satellite broadband service followed a couple of months later.

A resale property *should* have mains electricity and water already connected. The 'builder's electricity' temporarily connected to new properties, though free, is unreliable and not at full power. Our lights flashed when the kettle was on, we could not run the air-conditioning at the same time as the washing machine and power surges caused havoc with the burglar alarm. Builders will regularly disconnect power for hours on end with no warning and if the supply trips when it comes back on, your fridge and freezer will remain out of action until the next time you, or whoever is looking after your property, make a visit. It is advisable therefore not to stock up freezers until you are certain the supply is guaranteed. When the official supply is due to be connected to the mains you are likely to receive only about 24 hours notice, and they are most likely to use the contact number you initially gave to the agent through which you purchased your property. One day Tony received a call in Manchester to inform him that the villa was being connected to the mains that afternoon, and access to the fuse box was required. Luckily I was in Spain. If you are not around however you will simply be cut off. If you are not a permanent resident, the chances of this happening to you are therefore quite high. Also, be warned that the utility companies in Spain do not mess about if you fall behind with the payments for their services. They will cut you off first and discuss the matter later at their convenience (but only after you have cleared the outstanding debt).

Properties on completed urbanisations are usually subject to a set of community rules that are supposed to be designed to ensure the communal areas are not misused, and that standards of neighbourly behaviour are such that life in your dream home remains pleasant. It is useful to get hold of a copy before making any decision to purchase. Most people will happily accept rules for swimming pool usage, noise levels and antisocial behaviour, but there is always someone (usually English and male) who wants to run the community like a prison camp. This curtain twitcher is always on the residents' committee, tends to hold keys to the properties of absentees and has nothing better to do than patrol the estate looking for dog dirt, inflatables in the pool, improper drying of washing over balconies, household waste in the wrong type of bin and cars parked in contravention of some edict in the small print. The rule that drove me to distraction at Los Altos was 'No parking on the car park' – thought up no doubt by someone who regretted buying a garage. The community jobsworth absolutely hates not knowing everyone and all their business. If, like we did, you resist his blatant interrogations he will pop up when you are off-guard and try again. If you are selling your property he will be sure to find out how much you are charging and then discuss the price with his cohorts. When you sell, he will call in on the new occupants before they have had a chance to unload, present them with a copy of the rules, find out if they are living there permanently or renting the property out, suss out whether there is any money to be made doing airport pick-ups and key holding and, if not, he will officiously advise them that "under section 13c they are prohibited from unloading during the siesta and by the way they can't leave the van there overnight because there is 'No parking on the car park'".

I have to question whether people like this really should be on a communal development. They lack the spirit needed to get along with others and they wind up decent people who just want a quiet life. I suspect that they get a thrill from having the authority to tell a child in the paddling pool that she can't be in there with a ball. (They tend not to be so brave when faced with confronting a big hairy German. In fact the big hairy German will usually get away with it on the grounds that he does not speak English. The jobsworth´s inability to speak German will not be the issue.)

I think it is important to stress that the word 'community' when used in connection with a Spanish urbanisation should not convey to the reader any semblance of harmony. Community meetings have an unpleasant habit of descending into farce, and the fall-out from them can go on for years. The ruling clique will usually have discussed at length any real issues and stitched up the decision-making process long before any meeting takes place. This makes it very difficult for anyone else to offer a differing viewpoint. Tony and I quickly became disillusioned with the process and stopped attending; choosing simply to pay the required fee at the required time and to keep out of the way.

It is hard to understand why Brits who have previously only lived in relatively large houses in the UK think that they will be happy in a small apartment in Spain. Communal living requires a level of tolerance of others that some of these people just don't seem to possess. Why don't they buy something in the mountains well away from the crowds? Community rules are the norm in Spain, but Spaniards are generally very community-orientated, friendly people. There is no wonder that they don't buy properties near to Brits. In developments populated by Spaniards, the atmosphere is said to be far more relaxed. They know how to enjoy themselves in a group without being a nuisance to everyone else and the only community rule that is sacrosanct is that you should be quiet during the siesta.

It should also be noted that whilst community busybodies are great at policing the movements of other people, they are generally not exactly above-board themselves. Many of them do cash-in-hand work that they do not declare for tax; usually key holding and cleaning, and undercutting the local taxi drivers by doing unlicensed (and uninsured for business) airport pick-ups. They also tend to sneak in the odd illegal alteration to their own property whilst making sure that no one else gets away with anything that requires a licence.

Additionally, the Brits have a terrible habit of wanting to put security gates and keypads up everywhere without much thought given to access for the emergency services. Our apartment is now trapped on the inside of a gated area, which was open plan when we reserved the property. It has made access to the pool for the disabled more difficult, and if Tony had ever required an ambulance the crew would have been unable to reach us unless I left him alone, ran down three flights of stairs, opened the gates and stayed there to prevent the jobsworth coming out and closing them again. I don't even want to think about the consequences of a fire. The gates were apparently erected to increase security and to prevent strangers from using the pool; not a good enough reason for putting lives at risk, I think.

I did hear a couple of funny stories about pool rules, but the best one was about a pool which had a list of fun-busting rules as long as your arm regarding opening times, inflatable toys, jumping and diving and reserving spots with sunbeds. You would have thought they'd got it covered until, in a single day, two things happened which sent the community president apoplectic! Not only was a woman sunbathing virtually naked, but also in the pool there was a huge brown log cruising around like HMS Invincible – someone had had a shit in the water! In their determination to stamp out enjoyment, the 'sacred committee' had forgotten to request that people keep their important little places covered and that they refrain from using the pool as a toilet. I am told that these oversights have now been corrected.

Much as we loved the design and position of the apartment in Los Altos the restrictive rules, and the number of sad people dying to enforce them, had the potential to taint our enjoyment of it. There is no doubt that the community is well kept and is reasonably peaceful, but had the rules already been in place when we were first looking, we would have rejected the property and bought elsewhere; the parking issue being a nuisance, and gates barring access to the emergency services being the deal breaker. Contrary to my previous advice, I would say that the best places to find out such information could be the local bars – there are no secrets in Spain and someone is bound to know which communities have long running feuds, restrictive rules, access problems, or dictators on the committee.

Unemployment

Despite having a small income from the rental of the apartment, I had totally underestimated the effect that being unemployed in a foreign environment would have on me. At home I had come to loathe the bickering and narrow-mindedness of colleagues and the stifling 'thou shalt not contradict the management' ethic of my workplace. Having been a reliable member of staff for over 20 years I had felt that my life needed a complete shake-up. This determination was fuelled further by constant changes to the pension rules that had left my plans for early retirement in tatters whilst I was still in my early forties. No longer could I see the point in additional voluntary contributions to the pension scheme or in loyalty to the organisation. The end was no longer in sight and there was no guarantee that it would not become even more distant. How can a worker be expected to plan for a retirement that lies buried in some distant unspecified year? I was determined not to die in the service of the organisation I had come to hate and immediately ceased saving for a retirement I might never live long enough to enjoy. My shift in attitude from regular saver to someone who thought it was best to 'spend it now before it gets swallowed up in inheritance taxes and nursing home fees' was symptomatic of many UK workers' resistance to grasping government policy. Decent people like Tony and I had had enough and wanted some say in how our lives were run.

From the day I left my workplace I never regretted my decision to resign but, in Spain and technically unemployed, I began to appreciate the structure that work in the wider sense had given to my life. I suddenly understood why my dad was taking a long time to adapt to the closure of his business. At the time, I truly believed that he should be celebrating his freedom, but his view was that the days were interminable and he felt lost. After six months of living alone largely funded by my savings I began to question my purpose and usefulness as a person in the great scheme of things. I had thought that I would relish the freedom to spend my days exactly as I wished and to read until my eyes watered, but the sudden halt from frenetic days at work to such a casual existence was giving my mind too much scope to worry about issues that had never previously entered my head. My dad's attitude now made sense, and I began to feel guilty for not being more supportive of him.

To make things worse, Tony was totally unsympathetic and apparently unable to comprehend my negativity; this just made me feel more trapped and more negative. There were days when I genuinely believed that the only solution was for me to return to my flat in Manchester, to let Tony have the villa and to go our separate ways because he clearly did not understand me.

Moves abroad like this are possibly easier for the retired who, hopefully, have a steady pension income and can relax and concentrate upon adjusting to life in the new location, but the reality for many younger relocators is that there are too many people scratching around for a living in the same, often unskilled, areas of work. Most of these people work without contracts, are not covered for injuries at work and have no employment rights. Some people reinvent themselves as air-conditioning installers, locksmiths, television aerial erectors and property managers even though they have had no experience of such employment previously. The work of these people comes with no guarantees, and is often poor. The majority are not registered as self-employed with the authorities and are therefore working illegally, yet people continue to use them because they more often than not undercut the quotes of the legitimate trader. In this respect I was no different. The cleaning of rental properties was always something I would have been prepared to do but having looked into the bureaucratic process and cost of registering to work legally in a self-employed capacity, I understood why so many people took the risk and just did not bother. In the end, I gave up on the idea completely and continued to rely on the (taxable) rent from the apartment as my sole means of income. Before leaving the UK, I drew up booking forms, terms and conditions and a refund policy. At the apartment, I made sure that safety equipment was available such as a fire extinguisher and first aid kit. I bought items that I felt my customers could reasonably expect to be provided; I was shocked to discover that some apartments with terraces on the same urbanisation did not come with items such as sun loungers provided – I had presumed that one of the reasons people came to holiday on the Costa Blanca was to get a tan! Anyone considering renting out a property should realise that it comes with a level of responsibility towards the guests. Those who don't want to manage the rental process themselves will have to use agents or the local self-styled 'property manager', some of whom charge an exorbitant fee and others who are not beyond renting out the property behind the absent owner's back and pocketing the proceeds. It is also worth noting that one scare story making the rounds was that giving permanent resident keys, and money, to unofficially 'manage' your property could invalidate your contents insurance. It is true that Spanish insurance companies are notoriously bad at paying out (aren't they all?) and it was being said that the existence of duplicate keys held by 'friends', could be reason enough for them to justify rejecting a legitimate claim. I doubted the accuracy of the story because I would have thought that insurance companies would prefer the property to be regularly monitored and well maintained, but I guess it is best to check before taking out a policy.

During the first few months following relocation you seem to just haemorrhage cash, so it is important to build up funds before you move to keep yourself going, especially if you have no job to go to immediately. I had estimated that we had sufficient put aside to keep us afloat for ten months to give us time to settle and to find legal and reliable work. We had been hoping that Pauline and Phil could help us out by putting a word in for us with the property company but, after the problems we had had with them, I thought if they saw my name, they would not take us on. Anyway, we were getting well into the ten months I had allowed for, and Tony was now on half-pay and still being held hostage by our former employer.

I needed a fallback plan but I wanted it to be flexible enough to allow us some choices. As I had some experience of training adults and enjoyed this type of work I researched the possibility of teaching English to foreign students and found a company via the Costa Blanca News that fitted the bill. As a 'language home stays' set-up, the idea was to provide bed, breakfast and English lessons on a one-to-one basis. The company, quite rightly, preferred applicants to have a recognised TEFL (Teaching English as a Foreign Language) qualification. I didn't have one but, undeterred, I went in search of one. The Internet is a wonderful tool in the correct hands and I was able to locate a course in Sheffield that was to take place when I next returned home. One intensive course later, and armed with my certificate,

I would be ready to be let loose on any Spaniard requiring my attention.

It is important to be flexible in your ideas of what you are prepared to do, and the more varied your interests and talents the more likely you are to find something suitable. Too much time on your hands and no real reason to get out of bed in the morning will lead to intense boredom and see you on the road to failure. Unfortunately, I think we Brits are becoming too ´Americanised´ in our approach to life; our diets are terrible and we are increasingly unable to entertain ourselves. We like to shop in one place for everything we want, and we tend to be loyal to one employer and therefore are not sufficiently diverse in skills to 'up sticks' and go elsewhere. As I did, you can find that what you have been doing for the last 20 years is of no value or interest to anyone except your previous boss. I may as well have spent my entire employment as an inmate in a lunatic asylum (or maybe that should be 'service user in an establishment for the cranially disadvantaged') for all the use I was out in the wider world. I had become institutionalised without even knowing it, and it was difficult to come to terms with. In fact, had I never left, I would never have known, and that would have been a real shock when I retired, would it not? I had not thought about it previously but maybe that is why some people (the police and armed forces personnel in particular) find it hard to retire at the end of an entire adult lifetime functioning in one environment. It must be scary to suddenly realise that you have actually come to define yourself in terms of your employment – and that that definition has come to an end. The more I thought about it the more I was glad I had taken the risk and escaped. I wanted to be me – not what I did for a living.

What struck me as particularly worrying was that I had observed a certain element of the expat population by whom you can set your watch. They can be found every day doing the same things in the same places. They have developed a routine in order to get through the day and to overcome the boredom of a relatively pointless and aimless life in the sun. Obviously, there is nothing wrong with that, but drink features heavily in the routines of many and it is sad that lovely people are reduced to spending their afternoons in a fog of alcohol. After years in Spain most do not speak Spanish, they rarely venture away from the expat areas and have very little interest in, or knowledge of, Spanish culture. My over-active, under-employed mind would fix on these individuals and I would worry that we would end up like that. I certainly did not want drink to be a regular feature of my day. At times like this, I would try to pull myself together and think of something positive to focus upon.

Interestingly though, I have observed two categories of drinker whilst I have been in Spain; one group thinks they don't drink and they tend to look down on the others who, as far as they are concerned, obviously do. I refer to what I call 'bar drinkers' and 'balcony drinkers'. The balcony drinkers think that their drinking doesn't count because they don't go out to do it in public. They comment on the bar drinkers; "Did you see what time he was in there this morning, he's in there every day?" Yes, I think, and you are pissed on your balcony by about 5pm every day too, but let's just gloss over that, shall we? Drink *is* an issue in Spain and it is not the place to be if you have a drink problem, whether you do it on the balcony or in a bar. Not all bar drinkers are drunks, not all bar drinkers drink alcohol, but the assumption is that they do. As I've already mentioned, many people go to the bars to socialise and get out of the house. (Tony goes every morning to read his paper and have a coffee, he then goes out several evenings a week for a few halves; sometimes I join him, and sometimes I don't. It keeps him happy and that is how he has made his friends.) Yes, there are people who *always* go out and drink to get drunk, but equally there are many who are regularly drunk at home. People drink to ease stress and to fill time; it is an easy habit to adopt and a difficult one to shake off.

Making It Work

Thank goodness, the rental of the apartment served its purpose in that it gave me something to do and a reason to stay, but I realised after about six months that it was not going to be sufficient to sustain us in the long term and was not something I really wanted to do. My business sense was non-existent and I was getting far too worried about whether or not people were having a good time. We did well with the bookings we had, bearing in mind that the process was new to us, but I had competitively priced the rental periods and furnished the apartment to a high standard. In this area of the Costa Blanca the rental market is saturated and the customer has plenty of choice, so those charging top-end rents will find that their property is very likely to stand empty for a considerable time and thus fail to pay for itself.

In a way it was fortunate for me that I could not have returned to the UK quickly, even though sometimes I wanted to. I had made myself responsible for other people's hard-earned holidays and there was no way I would have let them down. I could have coped with the consequences of failure for myself but I would never have forgiven myself if I had ruined other people's expectations.

This commitment forced me to stick with my increasingly vague programme; otherwise I most probably would have followed the example of one of my neighbours and moved back before I had even properly unpacked. As it was, I was strangely glad that I had no choice but to stay and honour the bookings that had been made. In the beginning, as each of my customers arrived I would put on a brave face and tell anyone who asked that everything was fine and that I had settled; what they didn't know was that I was ticking each of them off my calendar and that there were days when I looked forward with high hopes and expectations of an imminent return to Manchester. I wanted to see the backs of my last customers and ditch the responsibilities and restrictions that went with them.

I was lucky to have marvellous guests and, in my brighter moments, this made the decision to carry on worthwhile. I enjoyed having them in the apartment and I was relieved that everyone enjoyed their holidays. Barring a few unexpected incidents; one couple missing their flight, another locking themselves out and an emergency with the hot water boiler, I was fortunate to get through the season without major problems or accidents. One of my best friends won the award for the most breakages in a week (all the items drink-related), but I never had to deal with cleaning up drink-induced vomit or the ruination of bedding through illness. The apartment made it through the season undamaged and this enabled us to get it on the market quickly when all our commitments had been met.

Providing that you have not made a really serious error of judgement, your situation can be turned into something positive. Although I periodically entered miserable phases, I vowed not to allow myself to return to the UK until I had achieved something in my own eyes (this did not stop me from thinking about it however). Previously, I had always been anxious to appear successful even if I wasn't happy. Now I had created a massive opportunity to satisfy my own idea of success. Having broken out of the stifling world of local government employment I wanted to be more adventurous in my work options and less tied to one thing. I still wanted to become a competent Spanish speaker and to experience a different approach to life. I met a diverse range of people who had had life experiences that were poles apart from my own; some were truly amazing and others quite frightening but they all made me feel that I had not really begun to get the most out of my life or myself. Lacking any real challenges in my daily life over the previous 20-odd years, I was unaware of the full range of my own capabilities and true strength of character. I had been cocooned in a false security that depended too much on the workplace I disliked. The removal of that security was simultaneously frightening and exciting. It also caused my appreciation of the things I already had to increase dramatically. I now believe that familiarity had numbed me to the things for which I should have been grateful. In some respects this realisation made me more homesick, but it also confirmed my determination, in my more lucid moments, to ensure the 'success' of the venture to my own satisfaction and no one else's (apart from Tony's). One problem was that even though I had had the attitude from the outset that if it didn't work out we could always go back, I hadn't considered what constituted 'success' or how long it would take to achieve it. Even the concept of writing a book raised my spirits; it was an unachieved ambition, one I had never expected to fulfil, but the door to it had unexpectedly drifted open. Opportunities like this rarely present themselves and it is important not to let them slip out of reach to become yet another 'if only'. Ironically, I made a start on the book on a day when I felt absolutely dreadful. I felt like packing a bag and abandoning Spain completely but instead I picked up a pen and began committing what I felt at the time to be the whole sorry affair, onto paper. In the midst of the turmoil, I often thought how ridiculous it was that I had achieved so much and taken such a big risk with my life and yet I was still not enjoying myself. Given that I wasn't, it felt important that someone should benefit from the situation, and writing the book was my way of attempting to salvage something worthwhile from my predicament.

What the majority of us fail to do is to leave some leeway in our plans for a considerable amount of adjustment to cater for the unexpected and unpredictable. It is almost inevitable that things will go wrong at some stage. Most of us set out with too firm an idea of how we would like things to turn out. When that doesn't materialise disappointment is almost guaranteed. We all want to be all that we have the potential to be, but to achieve that, we also have to be brave. What begins as an inspired and exciting adventure can quickly develop into a tense scenario that stretches your confidence and optimism to the limit. Only you can decide whether it is worth carrying on and if you have the strength and resources to do so.

When The Going Gets Tough
Don't Read The Papers

The local English language papers such as the *Costa Blanca News* are a godsend when you first arrive. They are full of information for the novice expat and if you need a dentist look no further – they are the gateway to dental paradise. Such newspapers also contain the English TV listings and a bit of advanced warning of the many fiestas and bank holidays that Spain enjoys. I have used the paper to find a car, get rid of an old suite and to locate the nearest dogs' home. If you are feeling good you will not notice how depressing they can be, but when you are feeling low they can make you feel much worse so, at such times, it is best to avoid them.

When you are feeling rotten, the only articles you will be able to focus on will be those covering land grab injustices, robberies, drug hauls, burglaries, parking scams, muggings, sexual assaults, property fraud, poor sewerage, poor construction and your common or garden routine rip-off stories. It will really gladden your heart as you try to adjust your mindset to what you hoped would be a 'better' life in the sun. In reality the crime is probably no worse than in the UK, but these papers don't report many crimes carried out on Spaniards, so it makes you feel like the expat element of the population is the only target and it can add to your anxiety. I used to be really critical of the 'rubbish' in British newspapers, but now I can appreciate that frivolous stories distract you from the sheer quantity of bad news and serve to dilute its impact so that you are not tempted to throw in the towel and top yourself. The expat local papers are not so delicate and tend to keep all the bad news to the first few pages, so as you sit down with your morning cuppa you can be thoroughly convinced by page six that *YES, YOU HAVE INDEED MOVED TO HELL IN THE SUN AND YES, YOU HAVE MADE A TERRIBLE MISTAKE!*

The messages from the majority of such news items should never really concern you, and they do forewarn you so that you can be on your guard (I however contest that I did not move here to be on my guard – quite the opposite in fact – I came to let my hair down). Just make sure that you buy wisely in the first place, and don't take unnecessary risks just to save a few quid. There was an horrific story about a British couple that were murdered by two South Americans who were posing as the owners of a property that they were only actually renting. The husband and wife were imprisoned in the property when they went to view it and were forced to hand over their bankcards and PINs. Their accounts were cleaned out and they must have suffered terribly in their final days together. Reluctant though I may be to say so, the large established property agencies at least provide some protection from such awful scenarios and the ever-present issue of land-grab in the Valencia region. By requesting deeds, or copies of contracts of sale from property owners, the agencies can go some way to ensuring that the properties they offer are legitimate, and most only show customers around developments on officially urbanised land. Do your homework, stay in control and don't rush into anything; there is plenty of property for sale.

Equally, don't do anything that you would not do at home. If you would not employ a Russian who came to your door offering to tile your patio at home, *don't* do it in Spain either. Hold on to your common sense!

However, if you are desperate to get out, and your partner is not and has to be brought round to your way of thinking, stick the paper in his or her hands and use the horror stories as yet another good reason for why it is time to leave.

July 2006 –
Don't Go Home 'For A Break'

When the going gets tough make yourself tough it out. Going home for a break to 'get your head together' is worse than staying and getting on with it. It solves nothing and can actually unsettle you even more. I knew someone who went home eight times in 12 months. This is too frequent and does not give the new location a chance to become familiar – it also costs a lot of money and erodes those precious emergency savings.

July was a quiet month for rentals, which surprised me. The charges for the apartment were very reasonable but the flight prices went up significantly, so I put the lack of interest down to that. In a way I was glad because the lack of bookings gave me a good chance to nip home to Manchester and catch up with a few friends. It was a big mistake. For the first couple of days I felt lost. There I was back in my own flat but with only a suitcase full of clothes. Tony was used to being there without me and had his own routine, which I seemed to be disrupting, and I didn't have enough money for retail therapy. I went to Sainsbury's and came out appalled at the price of food. I had become used to the Spanish markets and was disgusted at what UK residents were expected to pay for pre-washed, pre-packed food in miserly quantities.

I also found that I had very little time to myself to reflect on my situation; when you get home people want to see you and they look to you as though you are some sort of guiding light. They also either think that you are on a perpetual holiday and are living on Easy Street, or they analyse everything you say looking for the signs that it is not working out. You are therefore loath to say that 'actually it has been really hard and I don't know yet if I have done the right thing' partially because you don't want to admit that you are neither as tough nor as organised as you thought you were, and partially because you were supposed to be going to a better life and you don't want to disillusion anyone who might be contemplating doing the same thing.

Of course the people who *hope* that your life has all turned to rat-shit will *not* want to see you but they *will* want to hear all the bad news on the grapevine, so you are ultra careful about what you say in order not to make that sort of information available to them. Really, the best way to avoid this, and to reduce the stress on you, is not to put yourself in such a position in the first place. Keep your panics and fears to your most trusted friends or tell no one. Better still don't meet up with your old mates at all until you are really clear about what you are doing.

I didn't know all this at the time so please forgive me for not heeding my own advice. An ex-colleague organised a little reunion of about a dozen people, which I thought was a lovely gesture, but I found myself drifting in and out of a conversation that centred largely on the workplace I wanted to forget. Old issues were dragged up and gone over, and I began to feel really irritated and uncomfortable. During the following weeks, people wanting to see me, or wanting things from me, whilst I was back – references, advice, nights out – drove me mad. I must have had the same conversations about the same things a hundred times with different people and I eventually got to the stage where I didn't answer the phone.

To make matters worse Tony and I had several arguments, one of them very serious, and we almost ended our relationship when an old friend inadvertently, (I hope), created a bad atmosphere on a night out. It just felt as though nothing we did could go smoothly and I really did not know what the future held for us as a couple and the Spanish venture as a whole – not that Tony was part of the Spanish venture as the 'caring employer' was still holding his life to ransom in the UK.

It was during this so-called 'break' that I attended the TEFL course in Sheffield. Unfortunately, it started the day after our big bust-up so I hadn't slept and was dead on my feet. I don't know what I had expected, but I found myself in a class full of gap-year students bursting with confidence and enthusiasm for life and foreign travel. Most of them were heading off to South Korea, China, or Thailand and the certificate would increase their earning power. I just wanted to go back to bed. There were only two other 'old' people on the course and even they were more 'hip and happening' than I would ever be. Somehow I made it through the weekend by drinking gallons of Lucozade Sport, but I wasn't convinced at the end of it that any of us were any more adept at language teaching than the minute we arrived. Nobody failed – I think you passed just by attending for 20 hours without falling asleep. TEFL is certainly big business for those who provide the training. Having said that, the course was well delivered and not too expensive. I would recommend courses where you have to attend over 'distance learning' options, simply because distance learning is very easy for you to pay for and easier for you *not* to complete. At least an intensive weekend gets it over and done with in one sharp shock.

I learned another big lesson whilst I was back and it was that you should not underestimate the ability of your loved ones to look like abandoned puppies at the wrong moment. It will kill you inside but if you probe sufficiently you will discover that the only way they will ever be happy is if you come to your senses. No adjustment to their own lives will make things better – it is all down to you. They will be able to smell the right time to hit you with the enormity of what you have done to them – it will always be when you are already feeling low and unable to resist their solution to your (their) problem. During the first year, my dad resolutely avoided visiting me in Spain even once everything was sorted out. I don't think he could risk liking it and seeing why I might want to undertake such a venture. Life would be much simpler if I just came back. When I was at my lowest ebb I would agree with these views, but I also had to factor in Tony and how he felt. Tony is ex-forces and far more adaptable and adventurous than I am and he always kept saying that it would be good and that it would work out eventually. I couldn't deny him the chance to 'live the dream' if he was ever released from the clutches of the 'caring employer' whilst he was still alive. I was being torn apart. It was great to see my dad and to spend some time with him, but it was clear that he would be far more comfortable if I returned to the UK permanently. Even though I had not lived in my home town for over 25 years, I felt guilty for 'leaving' him in his old age (his assessment of the situation), and felt anxious that nothing should happen to him before I had time to make amends. He continued to be outwardly supportive, but he remained reluctant to visit me in Spain and came up with a number of inventive excuses to avoid doing so. I am sure he thought that if he spent more than 48 hours outside of Yorkshire he would drop dead! My brother refused to visit me on the grounds of his claustrophobia – he wouldn't consider flying and even the mention of the Eurotunnel would cause him to go weird

– so that had been something I had been prepared for (I really didn't want to see him pictured on the front page of the *Daily Mail* under the title 'Screaming Lunatic Escorted From Plane'), but my dad's absence did bother me.

In the end I was shocked to discover that I couldn't wait to get back to Spain, where most of my things were and where there were people who didn't rake up memories of the past. I realised that I didn't feel like I belonged anywhere any more and my internal struggle with myself intensified. I had entered a phase where it was looking as if it could go either way – 'Daddy or chips?' as the little girl says in the advert. The visit home had left me more muddled than ever, and I really wanted to restore some clarity to my life.

Luckily, August was fully booked and would keep me distracted for a few weeks. I vowed that the next time I returned home I would not tell anyone apart from John and Alex (who had by now replaced their clothing and were still talking to me) and my dad and brother.

Several days after my return I noticed that Maureen, a lady with two large dogs, from another part of the development, was conspicuous by her absence. She had moved to Spain alone and had lost a considerable amount of money exchanging her original countryside villa for the apartment she now occupied. (What I found even more distasteful was that she said she had also previously been conned by a retired UK police officer.) Additionally she had discovered that the pool that came with the property had no licence and that the huge shed in the garden was actually classed as a 'chalet' and also probably needed some permission from the town hall. She had been unhappy from the day she arrived three years previously and desperately wanted to return to the UK. The big problem was that she could no longer afford a property there and her solicitor told her that she would have to get the pool issue sorted out before anyone would show any interest in her apartment. To make matters worse, her very reasonable asking price of €145000 became a very unreasonable €170000 when the agent she had chosen added on his commission. No one had shown the slightest bit of interest in it; she was well and truly trapped. She had taken to calling in at our villa for a brew and a chat when she walked her dogs and her visits often ended in tears as she continually mulled over her situation. There was no doubt in my mind that she was seriously unhappy and in a terrible mess, and she had taken my definition of complete despair to a new level. I was just glad it wasn't me who was experiencing it ('every cloud has a silver lining' – to quote David Essex).

I asked around about her, but no one had seen her for weeks so I thought I had better check her apartment in case she had had an accident or done something daft. When I got there her car was missing and the place looked deserted. I pressed the bell thinking that if she was still around the dogs would start barking but there was only silence. In the end I climbed up onto the gate and saw that all her garden ornaments had gone. She had packed up and abandoned ship – so to speak. It seemed clear that she had become so despondent that she had seen no alternative but to just go and, even though she was an odd character, I felt a little sad that I was not likely to see her again. I could not begin to imagine what a drive across Europe with two big dogs in a small car was going to be like for her and I couldn't help but admire her for her guts. No one has heard from her since and her apartment is still up for sale with all her furniture still in it.

The abandonment of property in Spain is a regular occurrence. In July 2006 it was estimated that 10% of the property in the coastal areas of Spain was either for sale, unoccupied for the majority of the year, or abandoned completely. I suspect that some of those doing a runner are also the previous owners of the scores of vehicles that are left to rot and rust in the airport car parks. It makes you wonder just how bad this place can get. I hope that I never find out.

August 2006 –
A Change Of Attitude – Franco's Trays

I was told by a local resident that General Franco was supposed to have had just two trays on his desk in the place of 'In' and 'Out', which were labelled 'Problems that time will solve' and 'Problems that time has solved', because 'just give it time' was a phrase I had been getting tired of hearing even though I knew deep down that there was probably some truth in it. The people who used it always appeared to be happy and settled (though outwardly so did I, so it is true that appearances can be deceptive) and I suspected that nine times out of ten the phrase was just used as one of those meaningless throw-away lines that people fall back on when what they really want is for you to either shut up or change the subject. I tried not to discuss my unease with my situation because I found that it could actually trigger off a bigger reaction from someone else who was just about keeping the lid on their own issues.

However, the 'just the two trays' story had captured my attention. I wondered if Franco secretly had a tray for 'Problems which time has not solved', or if he sneaked a few into the bin, or whether he stoically just left them in the first tray forever. After all you don't know how long these things are going to take do you? And that, I felt, was precisely the problem with the 'just give it time' solution. The people who said it didn't really know how long the required amount of time was, so it wasn't much help. 'Just give it 12 months' gives you something to aim for but the concept of an unspecified length of time is too fuzzy to be of any comfort. Anyway, I knew loads of people who had had wobbles, doubts and crises and come through them. I had seen people arrive and depart again very swiftly, not having given it a chance. And I knew plenty of people, like myself, stuck somewhere between the two who were hoping to wake up one morning and feel that Spain was truly home. The relocation was certainly the most challenging thing I had ever done in my life and it had turned my ordered world upside down. I wanted to know for certain that it would all be OK and that I had not walked out of one unsatisfactory existence into another, but those reassurances were not available to me. Pat, an acquaintance of mine, was still having the occasional wobble after five years, and she surprised me even further by asking me (at that stage a veteran of seven months) what a 'denuncia' was. Did she not read the *Costa Blanca News*? It's a positive denuncia-fest of denuncia-filled articles to delight the most addicted denuncia junkie. She had obviously never had a proper 'Welcome to Spain'; her dirty knickers had clearly never been stolen! Even more worrying for me was the fact that she was still experiencing doubts several years in. Deep down I was becoming convinced that Spain was full of expats putting on a brave face and accepting the folly of their decision to move to another country with the usual British stiff upper lip. One or two people I spoke to were honest enough to admit that they would love to go back but that they had been too long off the UK housing ladder and would be unable to get back onto it with any style. No one ever seems to shake off the tendency to care about what other people think, and going back to a smaller house than the one they originally left would be considered to be a measurement of their failure. I too must say that I was loath to admit defeat at such an early stage because I didn't want to give other people the satisfaction of saying that they had known it wouldn't work out and that I had been mad to leave a steady well-paid job in the first place. I was already thinking the same thing myself and didn't need anyone else to rub my nose in it.

But I thought I had a grip of this 'time' concept and felt that I must have broken the back of it by now. I just had to keep going until it worked itself out. I was just two customers away from the 'Great Escape Back To Manchester', but I was no longer sure that it was such an attractive option. I had come this far and it had passed relatively quickly. Nagging doubts were still creeping into my subconscious but with less frequency than at the start.

One thing that continued to throw a spanner in the works of any semblance of success was Tony's absence. The 'caring employer' was still hoping that Tony would save them money by expiring before his sell-by date. All I wanted was for him to have a relaxing retirement away from the rat race. I tried to convince myself that at some stage they would have to let him go but the time it was taking was certainly taking its toll on our prospects of success and future happiness in Spain.

On August 4th he went back to see the company doctor for the fourth time and was told that the process could now stretch into October because the 'Inhuman Resources Department' might want another opinion. They had already had three opinions, but clearly had not yet had the one that they were looking for – that God would beam down a new set of lungs and he would return to work in full health. Had I been given this news a few weeks earlier I would probably have gone ballistic, but by now we were used to Tony being treated as though he would make a miraculous recovery if only we waited long enough. Franco's trays again – perhaps that was the method used by 'Inhuman Resources' – in time he might recover and get back to work, or become so incapacitated that even they had to admit he was no longer of any use to them. It would be recorded as a 'positive cost-saving outcome for the organisation' either way so we just had to make the interests of the organisation our priority and hang on in there. Never during his absence had any of the hierarchy seen fit to ring him to ask how he was and, so long as the process was being followed with no cost to the organisation, the effect on his personal life was inconsequential. Either way he couldn't work (their own doctor said so), and they wouldn't let him leave. By now he was on half-pay, and would be on no pay by the end of October. The financial implications of his absence from work on his ability to support himself were clearly not on the tick list of 'concerns' because they were never mentioned. Perhaps they could starve him back to a full recovery; a bit cruel perhaps but it might work.

I just resigned myself to a few more months in Spain on my own. No longer were setbacks having much impact on me, I was getting used to them. Something had changed in a very short space of time and as much as I wanted Tony with me, there was nothing we could do. Time would have to sort it out one way or another and I just hoped that those who had failed to respect Tony would be dealt a bucket-load of shit in their own lives in the not-too-distant future. It was no consolation to know that other loyal and long-serving members of staff in the same department had been equally poorly treated when they had outlived their usefulness; it just felt like the whole situation was out of our hands.

By now I had established some sort of routine for myself (exercise, Spanish language, write a bit, read a bit), which made the days pass far more quickly, and which renewed my sense of purpose. I had intended to nip back to Manchester for my birthday in September, guests allowing, but I found that I was no longer enthusiastic about this plan and thought I would stay and do a few things around the villa instead. My Spanish started to improve, though I was still getting the occasional odd look (I told one local that I was an umbrella) and the place very slowly started to feel more like home. All that was missing was Tony.

I substituted some of my now much reduced TV viewing for Spanish game shows, my favourites being *Ruleta De La Suerte* and *Alla Tu* (*Wheel of Fortune* and *Deal or No Deal*). These were great for practising Spanish numbers and letters, picking up new phrases and getting used to the speed of speech. My biggest difficulty in understanding the locals was that they spoke at a rate that was faster than Al Capone could fire a gun. I was occasionally getting a chance to practise on my Spanish neighbours, but my vocabulary was still quite limited and the speed of my recall from brain to mouth was not good enough to have a flowing conversation. I could tell when I was not making any sense because they would, very politely, glaze over.

I often wondered how they felt about suddenly having to cope with so many foreigners on their doorsteps. I suspected it had been an enforced change rather than a voluntary one as they had gone from being in the middle of a lemon grove with virtually no neighbours to living opposite a collection of houses occupied mainly by English speakers. I felt very fortunate to be living opposite them and I hoped that they didn't mind us being there, but I'm not sure that if I was in their shoes I would be too delighted about it.

Though the townspeople seem to be very stoical in their acceptance of the influx of newcomers and the urbanisation has been very well, and very quickly, serviced by the town hall, our presence has given rise to some unfortunate side effects. At the end of August our own supermarket opened; two weeks later it became a scavenging point for stray dogs and gypsies; the manager was robbed of the takings, and a woman was mugged on the car park. There is no doubt that such problems had not been an issue in the previously existing lemon grove.

September 2006 – Neighbours At Last

The beginning of September brought with it a flurry of activity. My final guests had departed and I wanted to get the Los Altos apartment on the market quickly, at a price that would allow me to simply break even. Money was beginning to lose its attraction and all I wanted to do was continue to offload stuff from my life so that I was not so trapped, or controlled, by material things. I felt as if I just wanted to get by in life without worrying too much about the future – this proved to be easier said than done as I am one of nature's worriers, and offloading the apartment became a problem I hadn't envisaged when I bought it.

I decided to test the market initially by putting the property onto an Internet website. I had decided to try to avoid using any estate agents; not having had any recommended to me who were charging what I felt to be a reasonable rate. The Internet listing cost only €149; I had to write my own description and upload four photographs. I thought the ad looked very professional, but I didn't hold out high hopes of a quick sale.

During the first few days of September I was still feeling fine, but the approach of my 44th birthday prompted a rush of well-meaning contacts, which rocked my boat. I had decided not to go home and, with no guests in the apartment to distract me, it was not long before I was feeling a bit aimless once more. Even though the strength of feeling was much reduced compared to previous incidents I still couldn't believe the turmoil I had brought upon myself. I realised just how simple life had been with a regular income, fixed hours and no real control over my own life. I had taken back control and it was proving to be harder than I had imagined and not as enjoyable as I had intended. This, I decided, was probably because I was not used to really surviving – at 44 I hadn't yet developed the skills. Modern life has a lot to answer for.

The birthday itself proved to be a dull, wet day. It also marked the first anniversary of Spanish property ownership; 12 months to the day the previous year I had picked up the keys to the apartment. My mood was gloomy and it poured down; I did not feel like celebrating and I was sure that someone up there had it in for me, but I couldn't for the life of me figure out why. Tony made me feel even worse when he rang to wish me a happy birthday but immediately asked if I would hang up and ring him back because he could not afford the call. Financially things were becoming increasingly tight, and in my newly fragile state, I began to fret about that all over again.

To distract myself, I decided to paint the window and door grilles before the winter set in. The air in this part of the Costa Blanca is quite salty and is thus very corrosive to unprotected metalwork. I had been aware for months that certain items of kitchenware were prone to rusting overnight if they were not cleaned and dried properly straight away. The items that were suffering the most from this were cheap goods purchased at the local hypermarket – they were soon discarded and replaced with items of better quality.

The ironwork on the house was a different story and had escaped my critical eye completely when I was supposed to be snagging the property. Many of the joints were already badly corroded and the house was not yet 12 months old.

The meagre layer of nasty dark green paint applied by the builder had proven to be totally inadequate protection in the areas where it had actually been applied. As I was cleaning the grilles prior to applying my first coat of paint I found many surfaces, not visible to the naked eye from a normal vantage point, which had not been painted at all. Not being in love with the builder's green, I asked my Spanish neighbour if it was necessary to get permission from the town hall to change the colour. He said it was not, though I also suspect he was not keen on the idea of a woman decorating, because a couple of days later, he began painting his own front gate and called me over for some expert instruction. I decided that my own grilles were to be repainted a lighter, copper colour and I was going to use decent quality paint. My neighbour had also made this point and, as I expected that my handiwork would be closely examined, I did not want to be caught applying an inferior product.

I had chosen this particular colour, not just because I liked it, but also because it was the closest I could get to the colour of the dust which regularly settled on all the external horizontal surfaces (and most of the internal ones if the wind was blowing in the wrong direction). I was hoping that the lighter colour would stop the dust showing up so much and therefore cut down on the cleaning. I started my task at the back of the house to practise my technique before I came to the notice of the 'Spanish Scrutineer'. The sun hampered my progress a little as it was impossible to paint when it was shining directly onto me. It was too hot, and the paint took on the consistency of toffee, so I spent my time chasing the shade. I also had to lift the windows out in order to be able to gain complete access to the internal surfaces of the grilles. This proved to be a pain and gave rise to yet another task of cleaning out grit from the window runners. During the process, the Spanish neighbour came over to compliment me on my hard work, and two sad, old, male and English 'jobsworth-style' neighbours (yes the Los Montesinos versions had finally crawled out from under their stones) came over to complain about the colour change. What really got up my nose was that I had recently gone out of my way to help one of them and neither could see my property from where they lived, but they insisted that there was a clause in the purchase contract that specifically prohibited me from changing the colour. I could remember being told by my translator that the colour of the walls should remain the same, but I could not recall any mention of the colour of the ironwork – after all grilles are not compulsory and I could have had them removed if I had wanted to. I was sure that I was correct and my Spanish neighbour assured me that I was (he also indicated that he thought the English kept their brains in small boxes). The unnecessary objections spoiled my enjoyment of what I was doing, and each time the police went past I half-expected to be challenged. However the police just continued to wave as usual and did not appear to be remotely interested in my artwork. I quietly cursed the English for their petty narrow-mindedness. Even more infuriating was that one of them thought he was now my buddy and kept pipping his blasted horn every time he drove past the house. This is especially irritating when you are stuck up a ladder and prefer not to be distracted.

Whilst the new colour was definitely more to my liking, it proved to be labour-intensive to apply, as getting rid of the offending green required three coats. In an ill-advised attempt to cut down on the number of applications I went out in search of a light-coloured primer to use as a base. The tin I eventually purchased indicated that its contents were white but in fact they turned out to be dark red and to smell like horseshit. To this day I am not completely sure what it was in that tin, but I used it anyway and whilst the first coat of proper paint went on more easily, it didn't save me any work at all. The whole process confirmed to me that the maintenance of a Spanish property can be a pretty tough job and the upkeep of those damned grilles is probably the worst task of the lot. I think I might grow to like the colour of rust – if I am here long enough.

I 'got away with' the colour change despite the moans and warnings to the contrary and later discovered it was never an issue. When our administrator was appointed in November 2006 he specifically mentioned wall colours, but said the rest was up to us. Had we had community rules (which at the time we did not) my situation would have been clarified immediately and I could have told the moaning Brits to 'do one'.

Towards the end of September, I was approached by a couple regarding the possibility of them renting the apartment for six months. As I was not anticipating a quick sale I agreed to the proposal as it meant that we would have some regular money coming in over the winter. I also secretly hoped that they would like the apartment so much that they would consider buying it.

Many people choose to rent for at least a year before they commit themselves to buying a Spanish property. Our new tenants fell into this category. They had retained their home back in the UK and had rented it out for 12 months to cover the mortgage, whilst they lived off their pensions quite comfortably at the Spanish end. In retrospect I think that their approach has been the most sensible and perhaps it is something we should have considered. This sort of approach allows you the flexibility to try out different property types in different areas so that you are more likely to get it right first time. Whilst we were satisfied with the properties we had, our satisfaction came about more through luck rather than good judgement. The story could have been much worse. However if you do intend to buy a property, I do think that you should set a limit to the period of time you are prepared to rent for, as I know of a couple who rented for too long and eroded their savings to such an extent that they no longer had sufficient money to buy the type of property they wanted. Equally, it is unwise to rent something that is far grander than that which you will be able to afford to purchase. The contrast when you start to view properties within your price range can lead to disappointment.

The very end of September brought with it a pleasant development in the form of agreeable next-door neighbours. I had previously been surrounded by empty properties and I had wondered on several occasions what I would do if some grumpy old bastard with a Hitler complex moved in. Luckily I need not have worried. An added bonus was that they also came from the north-west of England, so we had something in common to talk about which got us off to a great start. The only downside was that I started to speak more English than Spanish during the day, which led to the deterioration of the quality of my already less-than-perfect command of the local lingo.

Education

The beginning of September also marked the return to school of the local children after a whopping three-month holiday. Taking care not to overload the little darlings, the system required them to go in for half-days only for the first month to break them back in gently. After that, they went back to the usual routine of 9am till 12:30pm; three hours for lunch, and then back from 3:30pm till 5pm. Not being a parent, I could only imagine how difficult it must be to organise your life around such a disruptive schedule – never mind be able to work if you were ever lucky enough to find a job. Many schools put a limit on the number of children allowed to stay on the premises during the lunch break so the majority have to be picked up and taken back home.

My friend Janet's son resisted the return. Having been bullied during his first year he was not keen to be sent back into the firing line after a nice 12-week break (and who can blame him). Unfortunately this caused Janet untold misery for the first couple of weeks and she convinced herself that he would grow up to hate her. In the midst of all this distress she had to spend hours in queues outside the school secretary's office waiting to pay for books and other pieces of kit. By the time she had purchased everything that was required, her child needed a suitcase on wheels, similar to those used by cabin crew, in order to be able to transport all his stuff around without doing himself an injury. On top of that, she then had to traipse up to the town hall to renew his padron and apply for an official exemption from the requirement to learn Valenciano (the local language). The poor kid could still not speak regular Spanish (Castilian) fluently, but the school would not, or could not, excuse him from the lessons in the local dialect without the correct paperwork. All this was sprung on the parents at the last minute, so nothing could be done at a leisurely pace in advance of the return to lessons.

Other parents I knew were having similar crises. Many had put their children into local Spanish schools rather than the international ones in the hope that they would find it easier to integrate into Spanish life. After a couple of years (for those who lasted that long), the parents would come to realise that whilst their children had picked up sufficient 'street' Spanish to get by on a day-to-day basis, they were losing ground in those technical subjects where the language used was more complex, and their reading and writing of English was also deteriorating. One child who was struggling to keep up was put at the back of the class and allowed to do some colouring whilst the rest got on with the lessons. Hopefully, he will grow up to be a great artist, because he certainly wasn't receiving an all-round education.

In their eagerness to encourage their child to get to grips with the Spanish language, many people forget to maintain their offspring's proficiency in their mother tongue and overlook how they are going to cope with other subjects, such as science and history, that are presented only in Spanish from the child's first day at school. They are inevitably going to lose some ground no matter how bright they are. One chap whose van I hired for a day, said his daughter's pronunciation of written English was now done in the style of Spanish pronunciation, whereby all the letters are enunciated. He had been shocked to hear her ask her mother where C-A-R-L-ISS-LEE (Carlisle) was and he realised that they had taken their eye off the ball with regards to her English reading and writing. Many parents also find that unless their children make Spanish friends with whom they can spend the long summer holidays, they will inevitably spend three months speaking only English and their spoken Spanish deteriorates between school years. It's an awful dilemma – one I was thankful not to be facing as I was having enough trouble sorting myself out.

Luckily Janet's son had Spanish playmates on the urbanisation and he was also taking two private lessons a week. Unluckily, Janet could not afford private tuition for the whole family. The result was that she had a son who could choose to curse at her in Spanish and neither she nor her husband could be sure how bad the language was! He had also worked out how to get himself a few extra days off school when the mood took him. The local school has a policy of locking the gates precisely at 9am, so latecomers cannot enter. When this happens, the parent has to take the child back home and try again after lunch. Some expert slow timing by the child at breakfast would create the desired effect, and even if he had to go in in the afternoon, he would only have to do one and a half hours.

Another couple with a teenage son had made the difficult decision to send him back to the UK to stay with his grandparents so that he could retake his exams at a British college after he had completed his studies in Spain. He had failed to pick up sufficient Spanish to perform to his full potential and they felt that he was in danger of becoming unemployable in either country. He had already had to repeat one year and this had dented his confidence even further. In discussing such issues with others I was told that the problem was a very common one. One woman had never got around to putting her 14-year-old daughter into school at all. The woman had arrived in Spain following a divorce and had not bothered to register herself on the local padron. Without this she was unable to apply for a school place for her child, so she didn't bother doing that either. The girl is now in her late teens, does not exist in either the Spanish or English education systems (so no one is checking up on her) and apparently spends most of her mornings in bed and most of her afternoons and evenings hanging around the beach and the bars with her mother. As I have said previously I am not a parent but this does not seem to be much of a future with which to lumber your child.

It should not need to be said that anyone choosing to relocate with offspring should seriously consider, in advance, what they intend to do about schooling. This decision can be greatly influenced by the ages of the children involved, and the wrong decision can do untold damage to the child's confidence and future success. International schools, where English is widely spoken, exist where the expat population is already well established. Local Spanish schools cater for the rest and some are now very overcrowded. There is often a delay in the more remote areas in the provision of extra teachers and classroom space caused by the local councils' inability to predict the demand on the education sector. The influx of foreigners with children has increased steadily in recent years and it is very difficult to assess the age groups and numbers of those who will arrive as urbanisations are completed and properties are handed over to the new owners. The process is difficult to co-ordinate and the schools end up having to cope with virtually no notice.

As the number of young families choosing to relocate to Spain increases, areas that were more used to absorbing large numbers of elderly and retired immigrants, have found the shift in demand on the local facilities to be an unexpected shock. Inevitably, the parents of the local Spanish children have begun to raise their own concerns as class sizes increase and teachers struggle to communicate with non-Spanish speaking pupils. The mayor of a local town responded to the concerns of the parents of English-speaking children by assuring them that pupils who did not speak Spanish would be treated as though they were deaf and communicated with through sign language. It was the best he could do. Some parents responded angrily to this solution but I am at a loss to understand what their expectations were. Clearly they had expected the teachers to speak English, but they failed to appreciate that there is a large North African (French and Arabic speaking) population here too. There seems to be some misconception that we make up the majority of the immigrant population in Spain but, in fact, we do not. There are far more Moroccans, Romanians, Ecuadorians and Colombians here than Brits, and the Spanish are almost as bad as us in their reluctance to learn another language, so it should come as no surprise to anyone that most teachers do not, and probably don't want to, speak English. So be warned, you will have no trouble ordering a beer in a tourist area if you don't speak Spanish, but you will have significantly more trouble getting little Johnny out of doing PE for the day.

I think too many of us complain about the misuse of the system in the UK and then come to Spain and do exactly the same things ourselves. We don't learn the language, we don't integrate, we expect to be supported by the Spanish medical system, we dodge taxes, work illegally and fail to declare rental income. Even those who have apparently made a success of living and working here manage to conceal a significant amount of rule bending. We somehow feel able to justify it for our personal situations whilst condemning the practice in general, or we say 'well the Spanish do it' as if that makes it OK for us to do it too. Maybe it's something to do with the British psyche, but somehow we don't regard ourselves as 'immigrants' wherever we are – it's other nationals who are 'the foreigners' even if they are in their own countries. The best thing any parent could do for their child prior to moving is to teach them a significant amount of Spanish and check that their school of choice actually teaches in Castilian, and not in a regional language such as Valenciano or Catalan etc.

October 2006 –
Disasters, Dogs And The Language Barrier

October got off to a bad start and failed to improve to such an extent that I arranged the repatriation of some of our belongings back to the UK. My dad got the ball rolling by telling me that an elderly friend of his had been battered to death after disturbing an intruder. Naturally this upset him, but the knock-on effect was that he became more tearful during our regular phone calls and it was harder for me, on my own in Spain, to convince myself that he would eventually come to terms with me living in another country. A couple of weeks later, he disappeared for two days and I had to phone my brother to find out where he was and if he was OK. It turned out that one of his lady friends had gone into a diabetic coma whilst he was visiting her and he had probably saved her life by realising what had happened and getting medical attention for her very quickly. He had then spent the next couple of days caring for her at her own home but had forgotten to let anyone know where he was going to be. Immediately after this incident he rang to tell me that one of my cousins had committed suicide. It was someone that I had not seen for years but the incident initiated a series of reminiscences of generally happier times. I could not imagine how low a person's spirits needed to be before they contemplated such an irreversible course of action. It did make me get my own problems, temporarily, back into perspective.

To make matters worse, Tony's situation with the 'caring employer' remained the same and we were both, by now, totally disheartened. I somehow managed to rekindle my interest in the Spanish language and made major progress with new words and expressions. I would recommend to anyone that they learn complete, useful, phrases rather than random words so that at least they can inject some expression into what they are saying. However, I was soon to discover that my willingness to communicate with the Spanish population could get me into awkward situations faster than I could get back out of them. I was suckered more than once, but being duped into taking in a stray dog probably topped the list.

Despite having vowed to myself to have no more pets after Peanut died, I somehow accepted responsibility for a stray bitch on my way back from the supermarket with a bottle of milk and a *Daily Mail*. The farmer, who already had a menagerie in his backyard, had generously given it food and shelter for a couple of days and left it tied to the front gate in the hope that it was a runaway and that its owners would come back for it. Had I kept my mouth shut, he probably would have absorbed it into his collection but he saw me coming first. I must have 'pushover' tattooed on my forehead in Spanish because he spotted me from a distance and brought the damned thing out to introduce us. Before long I could hear myself, in inadequate Spanish, agreeing to have it at our house (without consulting Tony). Unfortunately for me, my Spanish was not inadequate enough for him to misunderstand me and the lead was thrust into my hand within a nanosecond. It was a sweet little thing but not really our sort of 'man's best friend'. In fact it was more like what Tony would call a 'Spanish rat', (possibly because apartment-living is the norm, small dogs are very popular over here). Tony likes something you can wrestle with and which he can take down the pub without his masculinity being called into question. This dog was not ticking any of the boxes, but I felt sorry for it and ended up back at the villa with a bottle of milk, a *Daily Mail* and a small dog (I may also have ended up with a guinea pig with no eyes but thankfully I did not know the Spanish for guinea pig and the farmer's grandson took it back in and put it on a high shelf in the garage).

Many Brits criticise the Spanish for the way that they keep and treat their animals, but I have seen no evidence to believe that the situation is any worse than it is in the UK, with the exception that a dog tied up outside in Spain is hotter than its British counterpart. Small dogs are popular and are treated similarly to their UK cousins in that they are family pets of the lapdog variety, kept indoors and indulged like any other. Larger dogs however tend to be tethered to some permanent structure outside and treated more like animals. Urbanisations populated by non-Spanish residents seem to attract strays. Those that are not micro chipped are invariably abandoned by their owners in areas where they know a soft foreigner is likely to take them in, or transport them to the dogs' home. Expats however are not free from guilt. Dogs are expensive to transport and some owners returning to their country of origin prefer to throw the dog out to fend for itself rather than to take it home with them. I didn't know which category my stray fell into, but I knew after only two days that she was not going to be a permanent resident. As well as receiving a complaint from a neighbour about 'that thing yapping all through the night' (a gross exaggeration), she escaped five times (twice back to the farmer) and I will admit that she did not appreciate being outside in the dark when she knew that there was a cosier inside alternative on the other side of the door – an obvious flea infestation behind the ears prevented me from giving in on that point. She was in all other respects a clean and well-behaved animal as far as I could see, though I doubted that she had had any inoculations as she was collarless and so displayed no rabies tag (I really should have been more careful but I didn't think about it at the time). A neighbour who had expressed an interest in her very sensibly retracted when she saw that I had been 'suckered' first, so I decided the best course of action was to find out if the dog had been chipped so that I could trace the real owner. The morning walk brought forth useful information from other dog walkers. They had seen the dog put out of a car several days before the farmer had taken her in, and a British man had been putting out food and water for her before she disappeared to our part of the urbanisation. Her wanderings were then curtailed as the farmer had tied her to his gate. As we approached a particular block of flats she became excited and wanted to be let off the lead – this turned out to be near to where she had been let loose and also close to where she had been fed by the kind Brit. I could also hear other strays barking in the nearby building site and assumed that this was where she had picked up the small amount of tar that was stuck to her coat. Nevertheless she happily came back to the villa with me, only to escape under the gate as soon as I took her lead off. Later that day we took a trip out and I had her treated for the fleas and scanned for a microchip. Not surprisingly there was no microchip and therefore no way of tracing her real owners. Having finally accepted that she had been abandoned, I decided that the kindest thing to do would be to try to re-home her. After a bit of phoning around I found, and passed her on to, a more suitable new owner whose own small dog had recently died.

After the dog trauma, October failed to improve. On Tony's instructions I had the balustrade builder back to give us a quote for a swimming pool, only to discover that his business partner had given up on Spain and returned to the UK in September and that he himself was considering going back in the New Year if the work situation did not improve. Only six months earlier these two guys had been encouraging me to stay, and saying how great life in Spain was. They were two of the 'give it time' exponents – the theory obviously had not worked for them. The main problem for this particular person was the overall lack of work and the large number of eastern Europeans who had arrived and were taking the work that *was* available because their charges were much lower. I went ahead with the quote but wondered whether employing him to do the job would be sensible; if he moved back to the UK and something went wrong with the pool where would that leave us? To get permission for the pool I needed a licence from the town hall and I also needed to get the pool added to the deeds. I spoke to my solicitor to ask how much changing the deeds would cost and after a delay of a couple of days he phoned me back with the exciting news that the deeds had been lost. Marvellous! The pool project went onto the back burner once again.

By this time I felt that the only way I could maintain any peace of mind was if I held onto the flat in Manchester for at least another couple of years. I might have to rent it out for a while, but at least it would still be there for us if we needed a place to come back to. We had too much stuff in Spain so I decided to scour the *Costa Blanca News*, by now necessary and compulsive reading material despite its wrist-slitting content, for an empty van returning to the UK for a reasonable price. I got lucky and managed to arrange the return of some of our excess belongings for only £350. What a bargain! My spirits improved just knowing that for once something had gone to plan. The

Manchester flat would be cosier for us, and if renting it out became necessary it would look less sparsely furnished than it currently did.

The very end of October finally brought a bit of good news. Tony's release from the grip of the 'caring employer' had been set for November 8th. It was obvious to both of us by now that the first year had been a relatively unpleasant experience and that the only thing we could do was write it off, have a good Christmas and New Year celebration and start afresh in 2007.

Land Grab Issues

During the last week of October 2006, the infamous Spanish land-grab problem raised its ugly head yet again and made the front pages of most of the local newspapers. MEPs (Members of the European Parliament), including our own Michael Cashman, were in Valencia to show support for the people who had lost land, money and homes under the much abused LRAU law. Unfortunately they never seemed to get any closer to a solution.

The LRAU (Ley Reguladora de la Actividad Urbanistica) regulations had originally been introduced in 1994 for supposedly legitimate and reasonable purposes: to prevent owners of large areas of private land standing in the way of developments or projects that would benefit the community as a whole. Such landowners were clearly most likely to be Spanish farmers so, contrary to popular belief, it was *not* drawn up with the sole intention of pinching people's holiday and retirement homes from them. In most regions the law has been implemented with very little controversy, and I hope all the Spaniards who had land taken in this way (and there will have been many of them) have been satisfactorily compensated. Unfortunately, it seems that in the Valencia region in particular the draft was badly worded, and this error was manipulated by corrupt officials, town planners and developers, to force smaller landowners to cede large portions of their properties for less altruistic reasons. Individuals who had spent their life-savings purchasing their dream retirement home with fantastic views and a large garden, away from the buzz of the towns and cities soon found themselves forced, by law, to sell off areas of their properties at less than the market rate, for the benefit of others. To add insult to injury, many were then presented with huge bills as their contribution towards the 'improvements to the infrastructure' they would enjoy as the area around them was developed. I fear that Mr Cashman may have been dismayed at the lack of progress the Valencian government had made towards rectifying such injustices after it was censured in a report dating back to December 2005. The Spanish just don't knuckle down and get on with things like we do when the European parliament shouts at them. They go 'Yeah right, so now go tell someone who gives a shit!' in a Vicky Pollard sort of way and carry on as they did before with a 'What you gonna do about it then' look on their faces. The EU Parliament says in reply 'We are going to come back in 18 months and we want your homework in by then' and the Spanish just ignore them. Perhaps Spain *is* the delinquent teenager of Europe and we will never get it totally under control. Sometimes I find this attitude quite refreshing; Spain does dance to its own tune and no one else's, and that is probably why the Spanish people are not crippled by stupid laws and have managed to retain their own national identity. But a line has to be drawn somewhere and clearly the innocent victims of this poorly-drafted document need to have the issue resolved; many of them are elderly and the strain cannot be doing them any good. Clearly the Spanish are adept at dragging these things out for the longest possible time and the continuing situation does highlight the lack of clout the EU parliament truly has if you just stick two fingers up at it. United Kingdom please take note.

I will attempt to clarify the situation a little for anyone thinking of buying land or property in the Valencia region, particularly in the countryside (but be aware that regulations here are constantly changing). There are three classifications of land – urbanised (already developed); suitable for urbanisation (may be developed in the future); and rural (not currently suitable for development). Most of the coastal areas where the dense building of apartments and villas has already taken place is urbanised and should be safe, providing the builder has all the correct permissions in place. Some smallish areas of green open space are left available for the local wildlife, and these are vigorously protected by environmental groups. Land classified as 'suitable for urbanisation' will previously have been classed as rural but will have had its rating changed to cater for predicted population growth and the need for further housing, schools and recreation areas. This is really the danger area. If all, or part of, a property, or its land, falls into this category and a developer moves in, nothing, at the moment, is guaranteed. It's like compulsory purchase with a dollop of misery thrown in for a little treat. It would be wise to avoid a property on such land at all costs until the situation is safer and owners' rights are far more robust. No attempts should be made to build extra, or larger, properties on land classified as 'rural' unless you are absolutely sure of your legal position. Equally, no one should assume that the classification of their rural idyll will not be changed in the future. In a nutshell, urbanised land is much safer unless you have a good lawyer and *you* ask *them* the right questions.

By January 2009, despite several valiant attempts to sort out the mess, little tangible progress had been made on the issue. The Valencian government was maintaining its stance – that there was *no* problem. The EU parliament was *threatening* Spain with a fine, and the Spanish, in turn, were slowing the process down further by responding with social, political and other environmental points, which detracted from the main argument. It is my belief that this matter will drag on for many years to come.

Unfortunately, this brings us to the next point. In the Catral area of Valencia many unsuspecting expats of various nationalities have unwittingly bought properties, illegally built, on rural land. These properties have been purchased via the correct channels – builder/agent, solicitor and notary. All of them have gone through this process, but none was informed that the status of the land was an issue. This cannot have been an oversight as the process was repeated for each purchase, yet these unfortunate people are in the strange position of having homes that were *legally* purchased but *illegally* built. Quite a few homes are now under the threat of demolition with very little in the way of recompense on offer. These individuals are not guilty of anything, and the removal of the mayor from office, due to the scandal, is of no absolutely no comfort to them. This is not technically an LRAU problem but thankfully Mr Cashman is on the case and hopefully he can finally get something done about Spain's inactivity on the matter.

November 2006 –
Trouble From The Comfort Of My Own Sofa

November was mainly wet and miserable, and it belted down solidly for a few days. The lemons certainly needed it, but the people whose houses were flooded certainly didn't. Our urbanisation got through the downpours unscathed, perhaps because we had the lemon groves to soak it all up, but as Spain does not have proper street drainage, the older properties in the tarmacked town centre were less fortunate and the streets turned into small rivers. Anyone thinking of buying a property with an under-build should make sure that there is sufficient drainage before turning the space into anything but a garage. Despite all this, I was quite upbeat as Tony was nearing his final date at work and would be with me for good by the middle of the month.

On the second day of rain I was sitting on my sofa minding my own business watching bored housewives' TV programmes when the phone rang. This in itself was a miracle, because the rain was affecting the satellite connection and the electricity supply, phone and TV reception were up and down like a whore's drawers. A guy I knew said 'hi' and then something about a job vacancy, and suddenly I was transferred over to an English woman who spoke at a million miles an hour and said that she knew a Spanish family who owned a fishing tackle shop, who needed cover for maternity leave and was I interested but I had to tell her straight away. She said this all in one breath and it was a lot to take in; I was just having a cup of tea and not thinking about fishing tackle. I didn't really know anything about fishing tackle and wondered why anyone would think I did. So I said I was interested and immediately thought 'why did I say that?', but being English I felt that I had already committed myself and found myself agreeing to an interview four hours later at the aforementioned shop, which was a 40-minute drive away, with a Spanish woman who did not speak any English but who would be grateful if I taught her some English in between my fishing tackle sales. I got out my dictionary and looked up as many translations of fishing tackle terms that came to mind and four hours later set off to pick up the English woman to whom I had spoken on the phone who wanted me to collect her from under a giant Buddha. This is not the normal way of gaining employment and I had not done anything to get myself into this situation, it just came looking for me. When we arrived at the shop it wasn't a fishing tackle shop at all but a rather swanky place that sold speedboats and yachts. I had the sneaking suspicion that the words for 'float' and 'landing net' were not going to come in very useful. The woman I had picked up from under the Buddha said "Oh isn't it a big shop?" in a tone that led me to believe that her link to the owner was tenuous. The place was a multi-level store bordering on a warehouse – the word 'shop' didn't really cut the mustard. It contained several expensive-looking boats and all the paraphernalia that boat owners with lots of money would like to buy. I could not see a pint of maggots anywhere. The woman who was supposed to be interviewing me was not there so I had to go for a coffee for half an hour in the hope that she would eventually remember that I was coming and turn up herself. Perhaps she was as nervous as I was. On our return to the store the Spanish woman appeared from behind a rack of water-skis. I introduced myself and she just smiled and did not bother to tell me her name – it was all a bit surreal and for a while I wondered if I was going to get out alive. I was 'interviewed' between a canoe and a rail of life jackets, with Buddha-woman occasionally chipping in for good measure. The Spanish woman pointed off somewhere into the distance and asked if I could use a computer. I could not see her computer or the packages with which she was expecting me to be conversant so I just said that I could. She did not ask me anything about my background or myself but wanted to know if I was prepared to do 'all the hours required'. This turned out to be most of my waking life with only Sundays off so I started to look doubtful. Buddha-woman then told me that other people had turned the job down for the same reason and that the Spanish woman was not likely to get anyone but that she desperately needed someone who spoke English. I started to get the idea that just having the correct number of limbs and turning up for the interview was enough to qualify me for the job. I said that I would have to think about it and the Spanish woman said that she would have to talk to her husband. I got the hell out of there and hoped to hear nothing more.

By now it was dark and still raining. I dropped Buddha-woman back under the Buddha and hoped to get back to Los Montesinos before the supermarket closed because I had suddenly become desperate for a large gin and tonic and I didn't have any in the house.

I arrived at the supermarket with only ten minutes left before closing, so I parked very close to the door. As I entered through the automatic doors I noticed a very old red car parked not very far from mine. There were four very shifty-looking men sitting in it just gazing at the supermarket entrance. I had a premonition of an armed robbery as the manager locked up and didn't really want to be around to witness it, but the pull of the gin and tonic was overwhelming. As I left the store with my drink my premonition changed, as the guys seemed more interested in my movements. I knew that a woman had been mugged outside the store quite recently and that attacks on lone women were generally on the increase, so I quickly got in my car and locked the doors. I was glad to hear them having trouble starting their car and I drove home via a circuitous route to ensure that they could not keep an eye on me and catch up. I think I had become a little paranoid as the good old *Costa Blanca News* had recently run an article on gangs that were marking properties with graffiti symbols that gave clues to villains about the occupants; elderly couple; lone female; big dog etc and I didn't want these characters to see me going into an unoccupied property alone and mark my gatepost accordingly. It had been a strange day – and I had never intended to go out.

Tony arrived on November 15th, which was great, but his pension had been cocked-up, which was not great. Basically even though they had retired him on the 8th they had not done the paperwork correctly. The upshot of it was that he would not receive any money before the end of December, and he would only receive it then if he returned to the UK by December 10th to sign another document. Luckily we still had sufficient residual savings to survive but the prospect of buying anyone a present for Christmas was looking slim. Anyway we were just glad to be back together on a fairly permanent footing and we set about making the villa a bit cosier to get us through the winter months.

Health

The end of November brought more anxieties on the health front and this time they were my own problems rather than Tony's, but the situation did serve to highlight something of which neither one of us had been aware. Many people think that because the UK is in the EU we are entitled to the things we had back in our own country when we move to live within another member state. Well apparently not. Luckily my problem was not too serious; I had simply caught a bad chest infection but even getting medication for this was not quite as straightforward as it was at home. The supermarkets in Spain do not stock any painkillers or cold remedies; the only medical supplies you can hope to find on your local supermarket shelves are plasters, tweezers, bandages, and surgical spirits. Any other medication must be bought at the Farmacias, and they don't tend to have large open displays of anything to allow you to browse and locate your preferred remedy. At a time when you are already feeling less than fabulous you have to hope that you are going to make yourself understood and get the thing, or things, that are going to make you feel better. I realised that we had been so intent on sorting out the drugs for Tony's condition that we had failed to stock up on items for routine ailments. In the end I was supplied with effervescent tablets of some sort (which failed to do the trick) and I was reluctant to ask for anything else, as I did not want to appear to be some sort of medication junkie. In the UK I would have just gone to Boots or Tesco and bought myself a range of painkillers, cough mixture, hot lemon, decongestants and something to help me sleep. What I ended up with was something akin to a vitamin C tablet. It took weeks to shake the infection off with the help of various kind neighbours who donated Lemsips and Strepsils to aid me along the road to recovery.

I have been told that the health system in Spain is very good once you have managed to get into it and that you can buy more drugs over the counter (without a prescription) than you can at home. The problem is that to enjoy the full range of healthcare options available you have to get into the system first and then you will find that depending upon your age and employment status you will qualify, or not, for different levels of 'service'. It came as no surprise to me to find that I didn't qualify for anything other than emergency treatment and that my eligibility for that could also run out. What did shock me was that I could also become ineligible in the UK – where I had worked and paid my contributions. Not only that but the entitlement could vary according to which region of Spain you lived in so if you moved from Valencia to Murcia your eligibility could alter; nothing could be taken for granted. The upshot of it was that, unless I had an accident, I was essentially a private patient and this, as we all know, can be very expensive. I could receive routine treatment by registering with a local clinic for a fee. This gave me the right to see a doctor, and I would then pay for whatever I needed. It seems that there is something in the small print of this EU membership business that has passed a lot of us by.

Generally it would appear that those women and men who are working and paying into the Spanish system, and those who have reached the official retirement ages of 60 and 65 are fully covered providing that they fill in the correct documents and jump through the right hoops. Early retirees like Tony and those 30 to 40-somethings who are just making an attempt to have a different kind of life can find themselves in a 'Healthcare No Man's Land'. What do they do? Many take the risk that nothing serious will happen to them until they are old enough. Some rely solely on the EHIC (European Health Insurance Card) for emergencies. Others take out costly private health insurance plans if they are still healthy enough to qualify for one, or they keep up the pretence of a life in the UK so that if it becomes necessary they can nip back and enjoy the benefit of their own NI contributions. Once again, those people who really want to do things officially and in the correct manner are the ones who are most likely to find themselves in the worst position. Early retirees, with existing medical conditions, who have declared themselves resident in Spain, may receive only two years' residual UK NHS cover and could then find themselves classed as private patients until they reach the official age of retirement. If their health deteriorates and they then decide to return to the UK they are likely to discover that they are ineligible for UK NHS treatment unless they can show that they have made a commitment to staying (for example by taking out a mortgage). If an early retiree develops a condition which does not constitute an emergency during their residency in Spain the situation can be even worse. All this was news to me until I was told about a couple living in the Murcia region who had come out in their late fifties and who had to return to the UK after only three years when one of them became ill. They would have loved to have stayed as they were very happy where they were but their residual UK NHS cover expired just after the condition became apparent and they had to begin paying for the treatment administered in Spain or it would have simply been withdrawn. After all their savings had been spent on Spanish medical care, they had no option but to sell up and move back to the UK. At the time, if this particular couple had lived just a few miles up the road in the Valencia region they would have fared a little better simply because the region has a larger and more well-established expat community. Because of this an agreement *had* been reached whereby early retirees received cover so long as they proved they were no longer entitled to NHS treatment in the UK, and they took the correct steps to register their presence in Spain. However, this arrangement was scrapped in 2009. Currently, in order to receive Spanish NHS treatment in the Valencia region, early retirees must register for a 'SIP' card and pay €90 per person per month into the Spanish healthcare system. Regional differences in healthcare provision are not pointed out to property seekers and by the time they find out for themselves it is often too late.

The problem does not lie with the Spanish system, it lies with our own expectations of what the Spanish system will provide, based on our knowledge of the abuse to which our own NHS is subjected. The Spanish quite simply do not allow just anyone to walk into their doctors' surgeries and hospitals for free treatment. This approach may annoy those of us who have always paid our way back home, but it also prevents their system from becoming overloaded with unregistered patients. The UK system is not a club in which you earn transferable 'brownie points' – but a lot of us think it is. It is a UK-based system for UK residents. It is not a distance health package for UK nationals who decide to go and live somewhere else. I think I am now fairly clear as to where I stand in both countries and I view the Spanish system as a mini-version of the one adopted in the USA. I really wasn't aware of it before and had made the same assumptions as many thousands of Brits. Early retirees and those who intend to work without contracts or without declaring their income need to beware. With Tony still seven years from the official retirement age, and his pension being quite modest, I was concerned that we might struggle if his existing condition worsened and neither system was prepared to take any responsibility for the cost of his care. We have never been ones to use the benefit system in the UK, and neither one of us had had much out of the NHS in our lifetimes, so it has been difficult to comprehend a situation whereby a man who has made the correct contributions for over 40 years can be ineligible to use the service he has paid into. That, however, is the case and how you deal with the problem is up to you. No doubt there are always exceptions, and rules are constantly changing, so once again I would recommend anyone to check with the UK Department of Work and Pensions for the most recent UK information appertaining to their personal circumstances, and to find someone from the Spanish region of choice who can provide the correct advice as to the healthcare situation there before any permanent moves are made. If you don't take advice from an official source you will hear so many conflicting versions that you will be no clearer as to where you stand. In any case there will be several forms to fill in and, as usual, you cannot achieve anything in Spain without an NIE number, and in some cases a padron (a much misused document which is supposed to prove that you live in a particular area).

One option I do not recommend is that you simply hope for the best and gamble that neither you nor your partner will develop a serious long-term condition. Too many Brits rely solely upon the EHIC only to find themselves seriously out of pocket when the worst happens. Apparently fit, local residents, Bob and Sue decided to have a weekend away on the Costa del Sol. It should have been a relaxing break but

Sue had a brain haemorrhage on the first evening and was taken into hospital in Malaga. Armed with her EHIC, Bob thought Sue would be covered, and she was – but only for the emergency. Sue's condition stabilised and she went into a coma, the doctors said her condition was no longer an emergency – it had become a long-term care situation and the EHIC was no longer valid. Bob could either pay for her to stay in Malaga, or pay to transfer her to Alicante, or pay to have her airlifted back to the UK. As they clearly had no Spanish NHS cover he had to opt to fly Sue back to the UK – the cost of an air ambulance with a pilot, doctor, and nurse was quoted at €21000. Bob did not have the money. Should he abandon his unconscious wife of 37 years in a Spanish hospital a four-hour drive away from their new dream home, or try to raise €21000 to send her back to the UK where they no longer had anywhere to live? Then where would *he* go? A local group used its influence to reduce the price of the air ambulance to £11500 and somehow Bob raised the money. Sue was flown 'home', and Bob followed a few days later on a scheduled flight. Now in his late 60's, Bob has found himself sleeping on a friend's couch. His house in Spain stands empty. You have been warned!

December 2006 –
Hooray, The End Of Year One!

With Tony around I relaxed a little and stopped counting the days. The result was that they all started to feel the same and quite often I would have to ask someone what day it was. The first year was nearly over and it was a great relief.

The run-up to Christmas in Spain is much less pressurised and has far more emphasis on the religious aspects than the commercial ones. Cards and decorations did not begin to appear on the supermarket shelves at the end of September and I found this refreshing. Posters were being put up in the local bars and shops declaring their Christmas lottery number and I suggested to Tony that we should start to get into the spirit of the Spanish Christmas by buying a couple. The Spanish are big gamblers and the Christmas tickets come in sheets of twenty all bearing the same number. A sheet costs €400 with each ticket having a face value of €20. It is normal for the shopkeeper to make a ten percent profit by selling each ticket for €22. I am sure in the UK this practice would not be legal, but in Spain it is quite acceptable. People with superstitions about certain numbers seek out tickets ending in a particular digit, and some shops are known to be luckier than others. We asked to buy a ticket from our local bar and the owner happily sold it to us and kissed it for luck. On our walk home we habitually stopped for a last drink in a small establishment with only four tables, and here we were met with a quite different response. Following my request for a ticket the barman looked completely aghast and went to discuss my request with another member of staff. The cook then became involved and all three of them stared at us from the opposite end of the bar. Eventually one of them declared that we could have one – but only one (at the time this was equivalent to about £14 per ticket so we were not intending to ask for any more but it seemed to be a point of principle that we accepted that there was a restriction on what we could have). The ticket was reluctantly produced from a carrier bag under the bar and the owner said that his establishment was known to be very lucky. I paid and immediately began to feel guilty – I imagined that the tickets were already mentally allocated by the bar owner to his mates and that we had now made off with some Jose Manuel's winning ticket. I prayed that it would not win because I did not want to go back to the bar to ask how to claim any prize money.

Just before the winter set in we decided to have the car serviced – the wheels were out of balance after 12 months of being driven through potholes, and the steering was pulling and vibrating alarmingly at high speeds. A local garage did the majority of the work but we had to drive into the middle of nowhere for the wheel balancing and two new tyres. Whilst enjoying a cup of coffee in the garage waiting area the owner decided to test my Spanish and I ended up having to agree with him that Wales was in England to avoid an international incident. Apparently, he had once been a long distance lorry driver and he was adamant that Scotland and Wales were in England and were not distinctly different areas. I explained that Wales was like Portugal and it was located at the side of England like Portugal was located at the side of Spain, but he was not having it and threw his arms up at my lack of knowledge of the geography of my own country. He went away for a bit and conversed with a large woman dressed in black who was probably called Maria, and then came back at me with a pencil and a bit of paper. He forgot about Scotland altogether and concentrated on the Welsh issue as I had unwisely mentioned in passing that Tony was Welsh and was fed up of people thinking it was in England – "It has its own flag and language," I protested. At this point, I wished the Welsh flag just had a few stripes on it like a bloody normal flag because I feared that I was going to have to draw one, but in the end, he just indicated that I was so wrong he couldn't believe it and I just had to agree with him. Luckily, the tyre fitter came in at that point and said the car was ready so the Scottish problem never was resolved. His idea of the make-up of the UK is not at all unusual and I think Tony is now also inclined to agree that he is indeed 'from Wales in England' – it's not worth the hassle of arguing.

Before we knew it Tony was on his way back to sort out the pension problem and I was to follow a week later. I had decided to go back for three weeks to cover both Christmas and New Year with family and friends. With money now very tight I was a bit worried about going out in Manchester and paying my way so I resolved to try to see people in their own homes for quick visits and to get round as many people as possible in the first week to get it all over and done with. If you think it sounds like I wasn't looking forward to it you would be right. One or two people seemed to think I was back to party but I had to make it clear that my dad and brother were my priority. Tony was expected to spend both Christmas and New Year with his mum in South Wales, so we were apart once more.

The three-week return was the longest I had been back since I had left for Spain in early January. This time

I was not stressed out and I really enjoyed myself. I was also apparently cured of the need to buy lots of expensive presents and too much food. Christmas cost me only £400, when it would normally have set me back nearer to £2000. Nobody noticed the difference and there was a lot less waste. Fantastic!

During my stay I received a final insult from the 'caring employer'. They had decided to frame and post my long-service certificate. With no apparent thought for health and safety (tut tut!), it had been despatched in a brown envelope. The glass in the frame had been smashed in transit and I cut myself as I opened it up. The frame went straight into the bin and the bloodstained certificate was shoved into the back of our junk drawer.

The three weeks passed all too quickly and I had mixed feelings about our return to Spain. 2006 had turned out to be a tough year for both of us for different reasons and it was not an experience I personally was willing to repeat, nor a situation I was prepared to tolerate for much longer. Tony updated his original prediction and announced that 2007 was going to be 'our year', but I was not entirely convinced that the heartache was yet over. One of us had to be right and unfortunately, it was me.

January 2007

We got back to Spain on January 8th hoping for a better year, but also with some sense of achievement for having survived the first 12 months without going completely crazy. Tony's pension lump sum had finally come through, and so we were financially sound once more. I also contacted Pauline, our friend from the property company, (Phil was no longer working for them but she had been promoted to the role of co-ordinator), to let her have our CVs in case there were any jobs going. She indicated that they were unlikely to be taking anyone on for some time, as customers were a bit thin on the ground. I thought that it was only to be expected for the time of year and we were not unduly discouraged as we still had plenty to do around the villa to make it more like a proper home (soon after though the company started to lay people off and another opportunity never arose). Pauline later blamed the programme *Tonight with Trevor McDonald* amongst others for the general downturn in business. Such programmes, highlighting the pitfalls of buying abroad, generally lead to a rush of inspection trip cancellations and for a few weeks she had very little to do and her own job was looking quite shaky. Some of the reps were shipped off to sell properties in Turkey and Cyprus until the situation in Spain picked up again. They were destined to be away for quite some time.

Generally, however, the year got off to a good start but I was upset to hear from Janet that her husband, Mark, had been caught over the festive season "Shagging one of the neighbours". This level of 'seasonal goodwill' had not gone down well with the neighbour's husband who had immediately packed up and gone home to the UK without a backward glance, but Janet wanted to give her relationship a second chance. With the neighbour now minus her own husband and therefore footloose and fancy-free, I didn't hold out much hope for a happy ending. Janet had been really homesick before Christmas as it was her first one away from the UK and the mild weather had made it seem very un-Christmassy. This new, and unexpected, development was something she could really have done without. To make matters ten times worse, her mum had caught 'emigration fever' and was about to sell up in the UK and buy an apartment nearby. With the benefit of hindsight it would have been better if she had told her old mum to put her plans on hold and stay right where she was, but at the time she really felt that they could recover from the affair and that everything would be all right. She was to be proved horrendously wrong but only after it was too late and her mum was installed in an apartment down the road.

Tony and I settled back down relatively quickly but a couple of weeks later he had a spectacular blackout in the middle of the village. It was similar to his previous one but this time it took place in a more dangerous spot. Luckily there was no traffic around as his legs ended up in the road. He broke his nose on the edge of the pavement and took a chunk of flesh out of his forehead. Two black eyes completed his extreme makeover. For several days he looked like he had been in a good fight, and I was irritated, but not surprised, to find that most people assumed that the new look was drink-related. He seemed to get over the incident itself fairly quickly but I was shaken, having witnessed it and then having had to deal with it. The effect it did have on Tony though was that he took time to reflect on our future situation and he surprised me by informing me that he understood why I didn't see Spain as a lifelong venture. We discussed the options and we both agreed that given a choice, we did not want to die here (a subject you don't tend to discuss when you are looking for a property); a figure of four to five years was loosely settled upon as being long enough. We agreed that Spain was to be regarded as an episode in our lives and not the entire future. Bearing in mind that we were already into year two, the whole thing could be over in no time. Yippee! I was strangely relieved to know that he was no longer ruling out a return to the UK and it seemed to make being in Spain more enjoyable just knowing that it need not be permanent. I felt as though I was no longer in a rush to undo things and was beginning to develop ideas for the future, but it was comforting just to know that the option to return existed.

I was distinctly unimpressed however, by Tony's announcement that he planned to buy a moped, as I knew I would be worried sick every time he went out alone. He refused to be deterred and I eventually had to accept that he was going to get one, and that one day he might fail to return home. Clearly he regarded this as my problem, and I suppose it was. He had chosen a local garage from which to purchase the thing and so I was required to accompany him to speak to the owner, which only caused me more internal irritation.

The move to Spain seemed to have released Tony into a second childhood and he was uncharacteristically impatient to have everything straight away, so the news that the garage required a padron did not go down well – we had not needed one in Los Altos to buy the car. It took a further week and the production of several other bits of paper before the padron was issued and five more days before the bike was ready and properly registered. The garage owner was really good to him and actually gave him a brand new crash helmet – perhaps he knew something I didn't, but it was a lovely gift. I made Tony promise to wear it as he had been told that it was not compulsory to have it on your head – just on you somewhere! I didn't believe the story, but it could explain why you see so many Spaniards with helmets strapped around their elbows. He promised, but I could hear myself saying "Put your helmet on" every time he went out. I was beginning to feel like his mother. The owner said (in Spanish) that it had to go back in for a service ('service' in Spanish) after it had clocked up 1000km. Tony, thinking he recognised a Spanish word, said "Oh si servicios" (Oh yes toilets), and we left.

The change of character was not unique to Tony, which in a way was a relief but in another way should serve as a warning to others. I had observed a similar but more dramatic transformation in Janet's husband and, believe me, the end result was not an improvement on the original. Tony appeared to have entered a phase of life that did not require him to carry any responsibilities. The fact that his command of the Spanish language stretched to ordering drinks and the bill (and saying 'Oh yes toilets' to bemused garage owners) only assisted his new mindset and I was frequently left at home to deal with Spanish-speaking workmen (when they bothered to turn up) whilst he played out on his bike. Inevitably the imbalance of freedom started to put a strain on me (I would have said 'put a strain on us', but I am sure he was oblivious to it all) and rather than doing more things together we were finding ourselves on different paths once more. I was disappointed that his joining me had not really made life in Spain much easier but by now my expectations were not very high so the effect was minimal. The only good thing was that, in contrast to Janet and her husband, we were at least still a couple on civilised speaking terms.

In all, January was quite pleasant for us but a chance meeting at the petrol station with Don, an acquaintance from a local pub, left us wondering just how bad things could get. Don had lived locally for over six years; he ran his own business and was pretty streetwise. He knew about our two 'Welcome to Spain' incidents and greeted us with "Hi, have you been burgled lately?" When I replied that thankfully we had not he said, "Well wait until I tell you what happened to us!"

He went on to say that one night as he and his family were all sound asleep some scumbags had gassed them with some sort of spray which had rendered them all unconscious for approximately 12 hours. During this time, the iron grilles on a window had been forced apart with a car jack, and the intruders had had a leisurely search of the family home for items of interest and value. At around lunchtime the next day he woke up with a foggy head to discover that the place had been ransacked. Luckily, neither he nor his wife and children suffered any lasting damage from the gas itself but the house was quickly put on the market at his wife's insistence as she no longer felt safe there. The gassing technique had been very popular with criminals targeting tourists in camper vans during the previous summer. The gas was sprayed in through the vents and the occupants would be out cold in no time given the confined space, but it would seem that the technique had somehow been refined to work just as effectively in houses. Having lived in a city with a high crime rate, I thought that no method would surprise me, but this one left me feeling that there really were no boundaries to the unpleasantness of human beings. Here was a lovely family, settled and happy and harming no one, whose lives had been turned upside down literally overnight by greedy thieves.

February 2007

The beginning of February was cold and very wet. Somehow the cold in Spain is even more miserable than the cold in the UK and I can only put that down to the fact that the houses are not built to retain heat and so you never seem to get warmed right through to your bones. I once again thanked God that we had invested in an economical hot and cold air conditioning system because we had the heater on in the lounge all the time. Once again I compared electricity bills with a neighbour, and theirs was a scary €200 more than ours. Janet even claimed that her Spanish friend had discovered that an extra charge had been added onto her bill – it was a fine of sorts. Her crime was that she had used too much electricity over a 12-month period. Janet claimed that Iberdrola had a benchmark measurement for the amount of electricity the average household should consume in one year; her friend was not in arrears on her payments, she had simply exceeded the benchmark and so had been punished with an extra charge. I found the whole concept bizarre, but not difficult to believe. On the one hand, the approach is very 'green' and, if it is true, it would force people to economise, but it is hardly a good business model if you are out to make a profit.

By mid-February, the sun was beginning to show itself and on several days it was warmer outside than it was inside. It was at this stage, with Tony's monthly pension payments now beginning to come through, that we finally took the decision to have a swimming pool built. I saw it as a step closer to a commitment to staying for a few more years as, up until that point, I had been very frugal with the outlay of any extra money on the property. We decided to have a salt pool because I had witnessed what can only be described as chemical warfare going on in the chlorinated versions at the height of the previous summer. The salt version was supposed to be easier to maintain and better for the skin. Tony also insisted on having a totally unnecessary springboard but I had to put my foot down when he tried to push his luck and told me to also request a slide. The company we had chosen was Spanish, so as usual I was doing all the talking and most of the actions. I had to jump up and down and say "boing boing" to order the springboard but I drew the line at miming a slide – you have to retain some dignity in life!

I had dealt with this company before, when my next-door neighbours needed someone to help them out with communication, and had been impressed by their efficiency and the fact that they went to the town hall and obtained the building licences for you. The whole process had taken only two weeks from plans to completion. We looked forward to swimming in our own pool by the beginning of March. Ha ha!

The architect was booked to turn up on a particular day but it was raining so he didn't bother. In fact he didn't bother for three more weeks and that was only after we had had two visits from the Policia Local. The reason for the police interest was that the lack of plans or permission had been no barrier to the arrival of the mechanical digger which turned up to excavate the area where the pool was going to be. The worst of it was that the digger broke the soil pipe and I had to tell Tony that he would have to go into town for his morning 'dump' unless he wanted to see the offending article shoot out of the pipe like a child on a water slide about 40 seconds later and remain on display at the front of the house (I for one was not going into the hole to retrieve it). Two days later the pipe was repaired and I really wouldn't want to go through all that again. Now I don't know if there is a law against digging a hole in your garden or not; maybe it is just the construction within the hole that is the cause for concern, anyway the police went away both times without getting too upset. What maybe went in our favour was that we had not made a mess on the pavement and the officer knew the constructor had built several pools in the area and was aware that the correct paperwork would materialise at some stage. I resorted to texting the salesman to alert him to the police interest and he turned up three weeks later, totally unconcerned and totally unannounced, with the architect. It was well into March before we saw them again. In the meantime the hole became a popular attraction for the neighbours. Those who knew us, blatantly stopped and stared at it, others slowed down as they walked past, to have a sneaky look. If we were around at the time most would feel compelled to come out with the startling observation of "That's a big hole". To which I would have loved to have replied "Oh so it is, I hadn't noticed it!" The follow-up question would then usually be "Is it going to be a swimming pool?" We always politely said, "Yes" as if they had miraculously hit the nail on the head from the endless list of options for such a hole from which they could have chosen. The question that always stumped us though was "When are they coming back?" Good question! Mañana maybe?

We had our illegal hole for five weeks, and had two more visits from the police, before the permission turned up and work started again. By this time, Tony had done another runner back to the UK to see his mum, and I was left to sort out the workmen (and keep them supplied with their favourite drinks). At the same time our tenants gave notice that they were moving out of the apartment; our steady income was therefore about to dry up and my suppressed obsession with estate agents was about to re-emerge with a vengeance. The apartment had to officially go back onto the market at the beginning of April and I had got to the stage where I just wanted the damned thing off my hands and the money back in the bank (preferably in the UK). To plug the gap in our income, I began to apply for jobs locally, but I never seemed to be fast enough. Positions were filled on the very day that they went into the papers or the shop windows. I tired of ringing places to be told, "It's filled", before I even had a chance to say what I was calling about. The only jobs that remained vacant were those that were advertised by establishments known to be poor employers; they either treated you like dirt or paid a pittance for a very long working day. Often you would see the same vacancy coming around again and again as people took up the challenge and then left after a few days. Very few employers offered contracts and therefore even if you were lucky enough to be successful you would be working illegally; for me the whole situation was unsatisfactory.

Some good news for Janet was that her mum had arrived and for a while she was much happier. The relationship between her mum and Mark was quite strained, but overall she acted as though a dark cloud had been lifted from her. It was lovely to see her so relaxed and it gave me hope that everyone who stayed until a certain magic time would suddenly feel a sense of belonging in this foreign land. Disappointingly for all of us, Janet's joy was to be short-lived as she soon discovered that Mark had been meeting up with 'the other woman' on a regular basis, using the woman's 12-year-old son as a go-between. By now 'the other woman' had moved to an apartment on another urbanisation, and had one of Janet's friends not recognised Mark's car, he might have managed to go undetected for quite some time. The negative effect on the whole family situation was immediate and things slowly, then dramatically, deteriorated between the end of February and the beginning of June.

At the end of February, I decided to have another go at having formal language lessons with a 'proper' teacher. My attempts to teach myself were OK but sporadic, and my vocabulary was made up of a strange range of words, as I tended to sit down and learn things as they were required. I could say, "The digger has broken the soil pipe and there is now a bad smell. I have banned my husband from passing solids so can you fix it urgently please", and after my Buddha-woman experience I still had a lot of fishing tackle terms floating around in my brain, but I could not quickly bring to mind a whole host of more useful words and phrases. Plus, I hoped I would only have to do the soil pipe thing the once and that that particular sentence was no longer required.

The previous February I had enrolled on a three-month Spanish course with a local college. Native Spanish speakers ran the course and it had been all right until it became obvious that, out of the eight of us in the class, some were only there to kill an hour or two and had no intention of doing the homework or learning the vocabulary from one week to the next. By about week four a couple of us were becoming frustrated by continually going over the same things and by week eight I had had enough and stopped attending. I decided then that if I took up proper lessons again it would be on a one-to-one basis. I should have gone back to the same college for private lessons but instead I decided to ring one of the many Brits who advertised in the local press, professing to be teachers of the lingo. The guy's name was Pete, he looked about 12, and had a tedious attitude towards those of us who originate from that dark area situated to the north of the Watford Gap. He only lasted for two sessions before I realised that my Spanish was actually better than his. Several times I had to correct his spelling and pronunciation; he did not like straying outside his prepared lesson so did not answer any of my questions and I was extremely puzzled as to why he thought the words for 'long pencil, short pencil' were a good place to start.

For the privilege of not actually teaching me anything, he was charging €15 an hour, which at the time was about ten quid. My mistake was to have assumed that anyone who was advertising themselves as a teacher of Spanish would be able to speak it fluently themselves. He had actually done a free course provided by the town hall, copied their lessons in no particular order and launched himself on a new career. He had only been in Spain 18 months and lived on an English-speaking urbanisation. Not wanting to hurt his feelings, I told him that I was going to be out of the country for a few weeks and that I would ring him when I got back (not). Call me 'Mrs Stupid' if you like but it never occurred to me to ask how well he spoke Spanish before I set him on. In the end I went back to my BBC *España Viva* videotapes from the 1980s. You can't beat Yolanda Vasquez!

March 2007

With Tony away and my movements being restricted by the presence of the pool people I began to go a bit loopy once again. I was so desperate for something to do that I read a book on punctuation and painted a room that didn't really need painting. I applied for a couple more jobs but was unsuccessful each time. (I discovered that most posts were filled by word of mouth so I really needed to get 'in' with someone who was already working to stand a chance.)

Our tenants were moving out on the 19th, and we had friends coming to stay with us on the 29th. Tony (in one of his expert displays of crap timing) had decided to renew his passport whilst he was back in the UK and it looked likely that he would be stuck there until the pool was finished, our guests had been and gone, and I had cleaned the apartment and put it back on the market. He would then roll up without a care in the world and ask me what I had been getting so worked up about!

To cap it all a new series started on TV called *Selling Houses Abroad*. It was very honest but a bit bloody late for several hundred thousand of us, and what really didn't warm my heart was the fact that Spain appeared every week – sometimes more than once. The programme featured cave houses with collapsing ceilings, houses that were under the threat of demolition, people whose services had been cut off, people who had lost everything and people who just wanted to get the hell out of Spain (forget the biometric passport, Gordon, if you let me back in I'll never leave again – I'll make do with holidays in Scarborough, and a job stacking shelves in Tesco). Occasionally, perhaps to break things up a bit, the programme covered a nightmare in another country but Spain was by far the clear winner of the 'Disasters in the Sun' competition. I looked at our hole/ pool and hoped it was going be OK.

Meanwhile *A Place in the Sun* was still going strong and guess what – I was still watching it – but now I unselfconsciously shouted "Don't do it!" at the screen (passers-by may well have thought the villa was occupied by a nutter, and they would not have been far wrong). I do feel strongly that the repeats of this programme should have updated market values subtitled over the properties and that they should occasionally include a feature on legalities and things that can go wrong – but as the programme is often sponsored by property companies that's unlikely to happen.

Four days before our guests were due, Tony's passport turned up and he arrived back. The construction of the pool had reached a crucial (and messy) stage, which ideally required good weather, so rain belted down for a few days just to wind me up. We had hoped the pool would be finished by the time our friends arrived so that they did not have to pick their way through rubbish and workmen to get to the front door, but it was clear that there was no chance of that happening; instead of swimming in it our guests would have to make do with watching it being tiled.

April 2007

Back on our own again – well, alone with eight blokes from the pool company – we settled down once more. The mosaic tiling had been completed after a bit of wrangling over the motif on the bottom. I was given a sample book and asked which design I would like. I said an anchor – the constructor said it was too blue – I said a compass – he said it was too big – so I asked if there was any chance of a starfish and he beamed a great big smile and said yes (I think I had finally hit on something that he had in stock). Filling the pool took almost two days because the water pressure was so bad. If you are not on builder's water it is advisable to get a tanker to fill your pool as it is much quicker and it won't lumber you with a big bill from your water supplier, but as we were still on the awful builder's supply, we did what everyone else had done and filled it up at the builder's expense. The pool was eventually finished eight weeks after the initial excavation, but this did not include backfilling the sides of the pool or finishing off around it so what we ended up with was a nice pool on a building site. We employed the same company to do the tiling and then another firm was going to lay an imprinted concrete driveway for us. The tiling went very well, but I started to have doubts about the drive when the guys who turned up to do it did not seem to have anything to do with the company whose brochure I had been given. It was probably a classic case of subcontracting but we both decided that we would just stick with it as by now we were tired of having workmen on the premises and we just wanted the thing finished. The process was very messy and involved them throwing powdered pigment onto wet concrete to achieve the finish we had selected. It was a good job that we got on well with the neighbours because, every time the wind blew, their property received a fair proportion of what was being thrown. The following day the drive was rinsed and the excess pigment went into the road and left a red stripe in front of our property (I expected this to attract the attention of the police but we got away with it). The colour was then sealed in and we had to wait another couple of days before a final resin coating was applied.

The completion of the pool had prompted people to start telling us their swimming pool horror stories and I could not help but wonder why they had saved these snippets until *after* the pool had been built. Of course, we knew we had to be careful as any pool is a potential death trap, but the story about a dog being found dead at the bottom of a pool that had been built with only one set of aluminium steps as a means of exit left me feeling sick. I had been very specific at the outset that any risks posed by having a pool should be reduced as far as possible. My major concerns were that we should have a barrier between the gate to the villa and the pool itself, and that we should have a handrail on the concrete steps leading into the pool. Too many pools are at shin height immediately next to the main entrance to a property, and I didn't want anyone (drunk or not) falling into ours by accident. We had a balustrade wall built to zone it off, bought a lifebelt and marked the depths on the wall. We also had a way out of it at each end (I am surprised to find that this is not compulsory). In the end, however, you have to decide where to draw the line between safety consciousness and gaining pleasure from your pool. Luckily, we didn't have to factor in any children.

All the weeks of hanging around the villa keeping an eye on workmen had caused me to become increasingly bored. Each day became much like all the others and believe me, as an avid reader, there really *is* a limit to how many books you can read before your mind begins to cry out for stimulation of a different kind (I managed to read 122 books in 2006). Equally, the lack of a pressing routine resulted in my not being sufficiently tired to get a good night's sleep. With increasing frequency, I was rising in the early hours and trying to find something quiet to do, and I began to appreciate why some pensioners get up at an ungodly hour despite having no job to go to. The result was that I secretly started trawling the Internet for work back in Manchester, and I felt that somewhere in my heart I had finally made my decision about living in Spain – I didn't want to.

Janet's situation was deteriorating rapidly. Mark was drinking heavily and rows going on into the early hours became a common feature of their daily lives. Their children were unsettled and her son was often too tired for school. She began to talk about selling up but her head was in complete turmoil and she could not think with any clarity. I was glad her mum was here to support her but worried about what the old lady would do if Janet went back to the UK without her. The whole thing was a mess and put my little problem of selling the apartment firmly in its place in the great scheme of things.

Things came to a head late one evening. Tony had already gone to bed and it was past midnight when I received a text from Janet saying 'goodbye'. I didn't know what sort of 'goodbye' it was – an 'I'm going to the airport' sort of goodbye or a more suicidal one. I immediately rang her and thankfully she answered. There had been a massive argument and she had set off in the car without the kids to drive back to Birmingham with only €400 to her name. Her husband and kids were in bed and she had left them a note. I tried to talk her into coming back – she was never going to get across Europe with only €400 but she said she was already up near Benidorm. There was no way I could catch her up so I had to just sit there like a useless lump hoping that she would come to her senses and return of her own accord. The following morning I went to speak to her mum and we managed to make contact with her. She had slept in the car and then set off again and got a bit lost before finding herself on the motorway heading back in our direction. We persuaded her to come back and make sensible arrangements for herself and the kids.

Urbanisation Fatigue

After 16 months of urbanisation dwelling I began to become irritated by living in a manufactured and enforced community. It is compulsory to have a community president (and on the larger urbanisations a committee), and the fact that the majority of us were immigrants meant that we attracted one another's attention in those first vulnerable months and this gave rise to the development of many superficial friendships. I understood the ethic behind it all but there were times when I longed for the anonymity you experience when living in a large UK city. I have never been one for going in and out of other people's houses, but I'm sure that boredom drives some people to become habitual visitors. On days when I was feeling particularly antisocial I would resort to sitting on the roof terrace and pretending to be out – otherwise I could end up spending hours talking to people I didn't really like just because *they* couldn't find anything else to do. They always used to show up just as I was about to eat, or watch something on TV and would generally put me in a bad mood and cock-up my day.

Budding committee members became my pet hate. You can recognise them a mile off. They have a residual self-importance left over from their previous lives and attempt to retain it by imposing their narrow views on others. They don't have to be on the committee to do this but they are far bigger nuisances if they are (the power goes to their heads). What they don't seem to appreciate is that, like everyone else, they have started in a new country with a clean slate and their previous lives hold no sway with their new neighbours. I had to bluntly tell one man that I didn't know him and he didn't know me and that consequently he had no influence on the course of my life. He looked stunned in a 'How very very dare you!' sort of way. I have found that those who regard themselves as having been 'successful' and 'important', begin to feel the impact of their perceived loss of status and they generally turn out to be the least helpful or supportive people. They are also the ones least likely to pack up and go home even if they are at the wrist-slitting stage because they feel that it will be seen as some measurement of their failure. On the contrary, I believe it takes strength to admit to a level of error and set about correcting it in the way that is right for you. Generally, the opinions of others are short-lived and unimportant.

Gossip is endemic on the urbanisations – some people have nothing better to do with their time, and misinformation is rife. Tony and I had vowed not to become involved in such cliques, but inevitably, this made us natural targets as the *subjects* of the gossips – the miserable couple on the corner etc. We didn't suffer too much (to our knowledge) as we tended to socialise with people who lived away from the villa, but Janet and Mark's marital situation no doubt provided hours of exciting entertainment and speculation, as some neighbours knew them and the residents in the next street knew 'the other woman'. One day I had to break it to Janet that she had lost her placing as the most discussed resident as what someone was having done to their property was currently causing a bit of a stir. The self-preservation strategy of some neighbours was to ensure that they were 'in with the in crowd', because they believed then that no one would talk about them, but as the alcohol-fuelled barbecue parties of the summer got into full swing someone would inevitably upset someone else and they would find themselves out in the cold. Such petty playground behaviour held no fascination for us and we maintained our distance as best we could (this could be difficult though and I'm sure we could now write the book entitled *A Thousand Reasons Why We Can't Come To Your Barbecue*).

Another thing that really irritated me was the obsession some residents have of asking people to bring things back, when they go home. There are not many things you can't get here in Spain (I have been unable to locate flat baking trays and Flora White cooking fat) but with some individuals you reach a point whereby you are reluctant to tell them when you are going because they will present you with a list of essentials for the return trip – the weirdest one we heard of was a request for a championship-quality dartboard of all things. The fact that you have limited luggage space and you might want to take something outrageous like *your own clothes* back with you never enters their heads. Similarly, you become reluctant to tell anyone in the UK that you are coming home to avoid receiving a fag order. I didn't mind John and Alex asking but invariably I received several requests – the damned things are bulky and you eventually have to start saying a firm "No" or you would be a) skint, b) questioned by customs and c) have no possessions of your own in your suitcase (but then I suppose at least it would be empty for the dartboard on the return journey once you had got rid of the fags). Tony hit on what he thought was a great idea to put them all off; he announced that he only ever flew with hand luggage and that it was full of clothes and essential medication. The upshot of that was that he had to resort to smuggling his case into the car under the cover of darkness in order to avoid offending the people whose requests he had refused. It is worth noting that, contrary to popular belief, you cannot take as many fags back to UK as you like from mainland Spain. The tobacco you transport should only be for your own personal use and should only be a reasonable amount for that purpose. If you are carrying several different brands, don't know the price of a packet of fags in the UK and don't have a smoker's aroma about you there is a good chance you will come a cropper at some stage. One guy I know took back rather a lot of rolling tobacco on a regular basis. What he did to attract the attention of the customs officers I do not know, but one of them challenged him to make a roll up in front of them and he was crap at it (it's not easy). The tobacco was confiscated, he had to pay a duty charge and the mate he had taken it back for refused to cough up for goods he had not received.

However, I digress. Another problem with new urbanisations is that it can take years to get an accurate postal address. Correos, the Spanish equivalent of the Royal Mail, is notoriously bad at doing what it is supposed to do – deliver mail to the correct address. If your local postie (if you're lucky enough to have one) goes sick then you get no mail until he or she is well again. If you are in a newly-built property, you are unlikely to have an official address for quite a long time so you get no post at all and you have to go and pick it up from the depot yourself. This process involves joining a lengthy queue with all the other address-less people, hoping that by the time you get to the front there is actually something for you, otherwise you can queue for ages to receive nothing at all ('Good game, good game,' as Brucie would say). After nine months in the villa we were allocated a street name but by then we had all made up our own addresses based on our plot numbers and the name of the urbanisation; Iberdrola had made up another version and our bank had created something even more inventive. To date there is still no delivery service, though the address situation has been resolved. I have discovered to my cost and inconvenience that the only task at which Correos is extremely efficient is destroying uncollected mail. They hold items for differing periods, and scrap them very promptly when their time is up. I am told that such mail is sent to Madrid for incineration. The mail collection point for the apartment was in a very inconvenient place and so I was not a regular attendee; to my knowledge, several important documents went up in smoke and I am blissfully ignorant about the rest. My last excursion to pick up something sent to me by the land registry ended in failure but, whilst I was waiting, I was entertained by an angry group made up of mixed nationalities demanding to see the manager because they all had three different official addresses but were still not receiving any mail. One woman's mail was being delivered to a chap who lived several miles away, who had an address that was similar to one of hers. Luckily he was an honest chap and had tracked her down and passed the mail on but she was worried about identity theft and the fact that a complete stranger knew all her financial details including account numbers and balances. The group was told to come back in two hours as the manager was having his breakfast (some breakfast), so I never found out what happened next. My *partial* solution to the problem was to rent a mailbox at a location that was more convenient to me. The mailbox had a proper fixed address and I found that far fewer deliveries went AWOL, but I couldn't do anything about the utility bills or the car insurance – I had to accept that it was pot luck whether I received them or not.

May 2007

May saw the situation with Janet and Mark come to a head. Sadly, they decided to split up and Janet announced that she would be returning to the UK in August to get her son back into school. Mark was going to stay in Spain and sell the house before moving on. The effect on the family was traumatic and Janet lost an awful lot of weight in a very short space of time. The news upset me but I also joked that I envied her for having a 'legitimate' reason to pack up and go. She and I talked for hours about our relative situations and we both agreed that your sense of isolation is very much magnified when your relationship is under strain. Janet's need to sell her property quickly meant that it was inevitable that she and Mark would lose money on it. They had created a family home out of the empty shell that had been handed over by the developer but the enticement of new properties is still hard to compete with. Having lived through the hassle of pool building and tiling and people not turning up for weeks on end to do what they were being paid good money to do, I fully appreciated the bliss of being able to buy a property that was ready to inhabit, but the majority of eager buyers would not see it the same way. The price was set a whopping €40000 lower than what they really needed to break even. As soon as the Se Vende/For Sale sign went up they received several enquiries but sadly, even then, many people were simply asking the price and declaring it too high without even viewing. The most common comment was "I can get one from the builder cheaper than that". "Yes you can," she wanted to scream – "but not with a swimming pool, light fittings, air conditioning, garden sheds, roof storage, bathroom fittings, white goods, phone line and British TV!" But it was no good, and deep down she knew that the price would probably have to be dropped even further. There would be a point at which they would be as well just handing the house back to the bank and walking away from it.

Within a couple of weeks I saw my friend become a shadow of her former self. She felt trapped, despairing that the property would take forever to sell (or at least would remain on their hands until the builder had sold all his plots of the same design). Unfortunately, her distress was contagious and I felt a strange panic bubbling inside me. Had I priced the apartment too high and would I ever get rid of it? Could I somehow persuade Tony that we should get out of Spain now and get him to think it was his idea? Within the space of two weeks Janet had knocked a further €15000 off the price of the house, leaving her with an overall potential loss of around £44000. This further reduction attracted a fair bit of interest, and she had several viewings in succession. *Two* offers materialised, one of them cash for a quick sale, but for some reason they turned them down and it was a long time before anyone even viewed the house again. The strain began to show in Janet's face and her hands continuously shook with anxiety.

Janet needed a van to take her and the kids' personal possessions back to the UK. I recommended looking in the Costa Blanca News for a 'van going back empty', and even set about trying to find one for her (thinking that I might get to repatriate some more of my own stuff at the same time). I mentioned the idea to Tony and he was surprisingly agreeable (perhaps I wouldn't have to do too much persuading after all). My increased sensitivity caused me to view things around me with a more critical eye, and I came to the conclusion that although Spain is undoubtedly a beautiful country, I had lost my ability to really appreciate it. As I looked around the urbanisation it felt as if I was living in an old people's home. The majority of permanent residents were retired and I had little in common with them. Once Janet had gone I would be the youngest kid on the block.

Van man arrived and I succumbed to the temptation to get a quote for the transferral of some more of our gear back to sunny Manchester. The price was too good to refuse and I booked him for early June. Tony didn't mind. Since we had emptied the apartment, our spare bedroom had been turned over to storage so it would be a relief to both of us if something could go and we could get straight again. Janet got a quote but did not commit herself; she was secretly praying for a miracle and just wanted Mark to walk through the door, say he had made a dreadful error and wanted to try again.

The last few days of May were frustrating. First the telephones and Internet crashed for a day. The following morning we discovered we had no water and moments later the electricity went off. We could not have a brew – and I do not do mornings without a decent cup of tea. The water was reinstated about six hours later but the electricity did not come back on. After ten hours I got fed up and rang Iberdrola and reported the problem in my inadequate Spanish (usually it just came back on after four to six hours without any calls being necessary). As day faded into evening, we were still in the dark with no kettle and no cooker. At 9pm, I rang again and said it was now urgent, "Ten homes are affected, and some of the occupants are *really, really old!*" I thought that would sort it, but nothing happened so we went to bed. We could not activate the burglar alarm because the back-up battery only lasted for a limited number of hours, so we were unprotected and completely in the dark. The next morning we still had no power. Two more phone calls were required before it was reinstated at 2pm. By this time, items in the freezer had started to soften and the fridge was warming up nicely. I commented to Tony that if he had been unwell enough to need his nebuliser I would have had to have taken him into hospital.

The rest of May passed without incident. Tony had a couple of his drinking buddies from Manchester over to stay for a few days and they really cheered me up. It was clear that Tony himself was happier with his old mates around him and it struck me that we had been daft not to factor in the importance of such people in our lives before we packed up and moved abroad. At the end of their stay Tony went back with them to see his mum and I was abandoned once more. I began to realise that the inconsistency of our existence in Spain was not helping with the settling-in process. I was due to go home at the beginning of June and I wanted to come back with a clearer idea of where I was going and what I was doing. I also needed to get rid of that bloody apartment. By now I had it on two websites and I also had an acquaintance from a large property company unofficially acting as an agent for me. Unlike Janet, who had at least had some enquiries, I had the square root of nothing to show for my efforts and I was already €400 out of pocket.

The warm weather brought out our creepy-crawly friends. Most homes had an ant trail somewhere on the property. Luckily, ours was in the gate-runner at the end of the drive and I was happy to leave them alone in case they moved to a less convenient spot. Our next-door neighbours had them at the base of their front terrace, not far from where they regularly ate their evening meals, and another family had them in their back bedroom. Apart from the occasional jumping spider (I have only ever come across these in Spain), and one enormous centipede, we were lucky not to have anything nasty residing in the house. I made a point of not leaving crumbs or food waste on any kitchen surface and we always did the washing-up immediately after eating in order to reduce the risk of attracting anything. We disposed of food waste daily and ensured that it was never kept in the kitchen bin overnight, and we shut the windows before dusk to prevent insects being drawn into the house by the electric lights. The bedroom windows had coverings that acted as both curtains and mosquito screens and we both managed to get through the summer without being bitten. Outside was a different matter but as we were scrupulous about clearing up drinking glasses, and because we rarely ate outside, there was nothing much around to attract any permanent insect trouble. Occasionally we would see smallish snakes slithering through the lemon groves, but I heard of only one occasion when someone had one in their garden (we were told that they were not poisonous but I wouldn't have liked to have taken a chance). The lack of plant-life and undergrowth caused by our joint aversion to gardening made our outside space a little less creature-friendly than most. The roof space was the area that caused us the most 'unwelcome guest' difficulties; the builder had not fully sealed the gaps at the base of the lowest line of roof tiles and this gave rise to a significant level of bird occupation and, further up the roof, small gaps between tiles were proving to be the perfect haven for a number of wasps. We decided to leave the birds alone in the hope that they were partial to wasps and would wipe out the lodgers we were least keen on; at least they weren't in the house.

Additionally, some unidentified animal life had taken up residence in our chimney. We had chosen not to install a fire and had blocked the aperture into the lounge with a piece of board – we could hear the 'thing' running around on it at night. I hoped it was only a lizard (a wasp-eating one at that), and that the board would hold so that it wouldn't fall into the lounge unexpectedly. I quite like reptiles but I didn't fancy the thought of one suddenly dropping in on me whilst I was watching *Britain's Next Top Model*.

The most unpleasant problem we had during the warm weather was a strong smell from the drains. The lack of rain meant they did not receive a regular flushing through, and as the temperature went up they became a bit 'ripe'. The odour was similar to rotting cabbage and was particularly bad on windless days. Those of us with pools had inadvertently exacerbated the problem by creating extra openings to the outside world via the plugholes of our poolside shower trays. Our roof drain and utility area drain whiffed quite a bit and this odour drifted into our back bedroom. I solved the problem by removing the drain covers and blocking the ends of the pipes off with plastic bags. The pool shower tray was given a weekly dousing with a bucket full of water containing a significant amount of bleach and I created an odour-blocking plughole cover from half a tennis ball. Much to our relief our next-door neighbours were also on top of the problem, but unless everyone around you takes an equal amount of care you are going to suffer (the properties that smell the most tend to be the ones that are not regularly occupied and maintained). Bad smells don't stick to boundaries, so whilst we succeeded in reducing the problem, it never went away completely until the temperature dropped.

Rubbish on the other hand was never a problem on the urbanisation, and once again I have nothing but praise for Los Montesinos town hall for its excellent service. The UK could learn a lot about rubbish collection and recycling from the Spanish. Our general waste was collected three times a week at about 3am (not once a fortnight), and the bin men took everything without complaint. We shared a large communal bin and the resident who lived closest to it did a damned good job of keeping it clean and smelling sweet. Large objects could even be left at the side of the bins for collection by a special wagon. In addition, there were several, conveniently sited, recycling points for paper, plastic, cans, and glass. They were emptied regularly and everyone felt inclined to participate in the scheme. Unlike in the UK, we don´t have to load things into our cars and haul them off to a town-centre location only to find that the bins are already overflowing and there is a fine if you leave your carefully-sorted rubbish at the side because you can't get it in. If the UK wants people to recycle, the process has to be made easier, and there have to be sufficient collection points to encourage the majority to take part.

June 2007 –
Home Again

My first trip home in 2007 was scheduled for the first two weeks of June and I had had a personal triumph in that I had persuaded my dad to come back with me to Spain at the end of my trip. He was only coming for six days but it was better than nothing and it meant a lot to me.

It was great to be back in my old flat. It felt more like home after the November repatriation of some of our stuff. I actually had clothes in the wardrobe and a coat hung up in the hall. The only thing that was missing to make the moment perfect was the rain. The first night was bliss, back in my old bed listening to the Metrolink thundering past, the vibration rattling my light fittings. It was absolute heaven!

Next morning I received a call from Tony who said I had better call Janet; she had been beaten up. If you have ever heard a human being in real distress you will know that it sounds like an animal caught in a trap. It was this sound which greeted me down Janet's phone. Mark had declared the night before that he would be out all night. Janet knew what that meant and had gone to the home of 'the other woman', to have it out with her. Janet's version of events was that Mark had held her against a wall whilst his girlfriend had a few swings at her, then he had thrown her outside into the gutter. She had a split lip, black eye, bruised ribs, and a twisted arm. Mark had threatened to kill her and his girlfriend had called her a 'dyke'. He had been drinking and later claimed that he had only been 'restraining' her but he made no apology. A neighbour had phoned for the Policia Local but they had left, uninterested, when Janet uttered the word 'domestico'. She had gone home and hit the bottle herself. If she had needed any confirmation that her marriage was well and truly over she now had it. She packed up all his stuff into bin bags and dropped it off in the car park of his workplace.

She told me she was unlikely to be still in Spain when I got back from Manchester; she was in a hurry to get out of the country. Amazingly, she said she still loved Mark and wanted him back but that he obviously did not love her. Her Spanish friend had suggested that she should report him and have him deported, (as well as the assault he was, at the time, working illegally), but she refused. Over the next few days, I kept in touch and she organised a van, somewhere to live, her son's enrolment in a new school, and a job interview with her old employer. My heart ached for her – she really had lost everything apart from her kids. She took to carrying their passports around so that Mark could not abscond with them. I never said it but, if he had had such a thing in mind, he could have just taken them elsewhere in Spain and she would have had trouble finding them; it's a big country.

A couple of days later my van arrived with our stuff and the flat felt even better when lots of little things were back in their rightful places. The familiarity of my surroundings and the rain battering the doors to the balcony were sheer bliss. By Thursday I was absolutely convinced that this was the right place for me to have been all along and I wanted to be back by Christmas. It was a new goal. I bought a *Manchester Evening News* and started looking for a job. The jobs section surprised me; it was packed with jobs I

found interesting. After 18 months of nothing but 'waiter/
waitress,' 'experienced salesperson required,' and 'mature
hairdresser' ads, I felt like a kid in a sweetshop. It would
have been easy to take just anything and get back into a
rut so I took a large step backwards and weighed up the
situation. Ideally I wanted a job with shifts that would allow
me sufficient free time to still make good use of the villa.
I didn't want to impose a move on Tony, preferring him to
have the option of continuing to spend a large proportion
of his time in Spain, to concentrate on improving his health
and generally to enjoy the freedom of his retirement. I
eventually found two jobs on the Internet, which fitted the
bill. I dithered a little too long and missed the deadline for
one, but the other was still available. The application form
came a couple of days later and I immediately filled it in and
sent it back. It felt right and I began to build my hopes up.

The return journey with my dad loomed, and the press
was full of stories of impending chaos at Spanish airports
caused by new security checks. Apparently we were all going
to have to start filling in some sort of entry form giving our
passport details etc. We were due to fly into Alicante on the
second day of this new scheme and I expected to be caught
up in a long queue of impatient, sweaty people – not the
impression I wanted my dad to get of the 'look how easy it
is to get back and forth to Spain' yarn I had been spinning
him. As it was I can only assume that day one had been so
hard to administer that the Spanish had abandoned the idea,
because we didn't even have to wait for the usual cursory
passport check. The worst thing my Dad experienced was
having to pay £7.50 for two drinks at Manchester airport.

To my relief he loved his time in Spain and said he did
not rule out a return visit. What a momentous breakthrough!
We never mentioned the strange marks on the front door
left by the maniac who had hacked at it the previous year

and neither did he. I made sure that all our meals were sufficiently British for him to appreciate that we were not going to starve to death owing to a lack of baked beans, and he also found himself a few local youngsters with whom to play football, using a section of the supermarket wall as a goal. On top of all this he could watch *CSI* and *Judge Judy* (programmes to which he seems to be addicted), albeit an hour later than usual – what more could a man want?

Tony, who was due to attend some wedding extravaganza in Bedfordshire with his mum, accompanied him on his return journey when his six days came to an end. We had not wanted him to get worked up about travelling alone (I feared that he would end up in Timbuktu) so we had organised things so that he had one of us with him in both directions.

I was alone again once more but no longer as anxious about the future. I had my job application in and my dad's mind was finally at rest over my living conditions. Janet was still here and was planning to leave in early July. She had sent her share of the furniture, and one of her kids, back to the UK and was living in a virtually empty house with the other child and the dog (which was not going back – but more of that later).

July 2007 –
Goodbye Janet

July arrived and the temperature began to rise. Janet had set her departure date and was going through the same mental turmoil she had experienced when she first came out. Each day as she called for a chat and a cuppa she displayed a different emotion and had a different point of view – she still hated him, she still loved him, she couldn't wait to leave, she didn't want to leave, it had never been her dream, now her dream was over, she never wanted to set foot in Spain again, she would be back within two years. I backed her up on everything – she just needed some support and to get the whole thing off her chest – but it was exhausting. One major thing that was still causing her to worry was the welfare of the dog and (I'm sure you know what's coming next) I knew that somehow we would end up in the middle of another dog trauma.

Hoover was a 12-year-old black Labrador. Technically, he was Mark's and although Janet did not want to take the dog with her, neither did she did want him moving in with 'the other woman'. I pointed out that once she had gone, Hoover would be in the house all day on his own and it was July and therefore very hot. She said Mark would feed him if we would let him out and take him for walks. I said we would, but questioned why did they not just leave such a large dog outside anyway. She replied that she did not want him to be stolen. I had not heard of any dog-napping; in fact dogs were more likely to be abandoned, but given her overall state of mind, I was unwilling to argue any further. Several days later we were to assume dog walking and toilet duties, and boy, could this dog dump for England!

The days settled down and I checked my e-mails every day, hoping for one inviting me to attend an interview in Manchester to appear. Just having the application in had made me calmer about the whole situation and Tony breathed a (temporary) sigh of relief. As the temperature steadily rose, the pool became a godsend, and daily swimming sessions led to me feeling far more fit and relaxed than I had for a long time. Tony settled into his own routine and the days just seemed to fly by.

Janet's departure loomed and I wasn't sure how I was going to react but she had one grand finale of a domestico with Mark the night before she left and in the end I think we were all glad that that chapter was finally over – for us as well as for them.

Tony and I cared for Hoover for less than a week before we had to ask Mark to find a better arrangement for him. We could see that he was becoming depressed and the poor thing didn't have a clue what was going on. He was hardly eating and what he did eat was going straight through him. We felt that he would quickly die of a broken heart if nothing was done for him. Within days of moving in with Mark and 'the other woman', he was back to his old bouncy self. In fact he loved 'the other woman' and got his sparkle back. Clearly it had been unwise for Janet to use him as a pawn in the marital break-up game and although I felt that we had maybe let her down in some way I also felt that the outcome justified our actions. It took me a couple of days to tell her where he had gone and the silence down the phone let me know how disappointed she was – but I was past caring.

Relocators should think long and hard about their pets; it may be kinder to re-home them in the UK rather than to drag them all the way to a hot country. It is an expensive business. On the many occasions when the move fails to work out, money can already be tight and pets end up very low on the priority list. Hoover is a lovely old dog and luckily he still has his 'dad' with him but the story ends much less happily for many others.

August 2007 –
An Interview For A Return To The Rat Race

At the beginning of August I finally accepted that if I was determined to sell the apartment independently it would take a long time. No boards seemed to be coming down and there were definitely more going up. The competition was fierce and we were now up against some desperate sellers who were practically offering to pay someone to take their properties off their hands. Our apartment was, by now, featured on two websites (at the joint cost of €400) and I had paid a 'special offer price' of €250 to have a small advertisement in property magazine. I was already €650 down with not one jot of interest to show for it. Tony and I had a chat and decided that we would have to cave in and go with an agent. Once again I was on the trail of an agent with a heart. Rather over-optimistically I re-contacted the big three to check that their rates had not been altered to reflect the depressed market. At 18%, 12% and "We won't tell you what we charge, we just put it on the asking price and the buyer pays", they clearly had not – and this didn't include taxes and solicitors' fees. Finally, Janet's Spanish agent tempted us. At 5% for the English and 3% for the Spanish it was a bit unfair but still very competitive. I asked why the two different charges and he quite simply said "Because the English have more money". I said jokingly "But Tony is Welsh," and he said "Ah, but Wales is in England." I didn't want to have that argument again so I let it go. We were inclined to give him a shot at selling for us because in the time Janet had been trying to sell her property, (through four agents) he was the only one to have arranged any viewings and he had managed to achieve two offers very close to the asking price. Had Janet and Mark accepted either of them they would have been about €60000 out of pocket at the end of the process. I hoped the agent could work some magic on the apartment because I was beginning to view it as a millstone around our necks. We agreed a price that would fall into most of the search results on his website to increase the potential for viewings, and I was also hopeful that he could rustle up some Spanish viewers and increase our potential customer base even more.

One of the problems with trying to sell a place yourself is that you limit the type of customer you can deal with because of your own shortcomings. I made the mistake of putting up a 'Se Vende' sign with my Spanish mobile number on it, and I lost out on some enquiries because callers expected me to be Spanish. They hung up immediately when they discovered I was not. Independent sellers would find it easier, and less frustrating, if they put up a sign that said 'For Sale' in their own language.

I happily handed Pedro, the agent, a set of keys and left him to it. Getting rid of the apartment was becoming a bit of an issue for us, I was trying to act as though we weren't desperate sellers but the truth was that money was going out faster than it was coming in. I estimated that we could last another twelve to eighteen months before we were in financial trouble. The result of it all was that simply nothing was going to plan, and whilst I blamed nobody but myself for the situation we were in, I did feel that we had been deliberately misled. Our decisions had been made based on dubious information. We had not known it was dubious and we had relied on it. I would like to believe that nobody had actually told us a barefaced lie, but I felt that the stark truth had been conveniently overlooked during the 'dream-selling' process. The actions of some had left me feeling very disappointed but the person I was really disappointed in was me. I felt gullible, guilty and conned all at the same time, and it was not pleasant. My guilt haunted me in the night and often I would get up in the early hours to write or do some housework. My body clock was all over the place and my own internal fight was mentally and physically draining me.

A few days later I was cheered up considerably by the arrival of an e-mail inviting me for an interview back in Manchester. I couldn't wait and booked my return flight immediately. The money was not that good, but it would keep our heads above water and I believed that the shifts would enable me to return to Spain on a regular basis (I had assumed this because of the availability of cheap flights, but the fact is that they are no longer that cheap and I was silly to think that it was a viable idea). I didn't dare to presume that I would be successful, but I prayed that, at last, there might be some light at the end of the tunnel. We decided not to tell anyone in case nothing came of it. I didn't want to get my dad's hopes up for no reason and I had to be realistic and acknowledge that as an overweight woman in my mid-forties I might not compare favourably with the bright young things who had also applied.

August continued to get hotter and breezier. Fighting the dust around the house was a lost cause. We liked the fresh air in the house, but not the rubbish that blew in with it. The local dogs were all having haircuts to keep their temperatures down and a few of them looked like they could do with being vacuumed too. I hate dirt in the house, and the grit and grime was getting on my nerves;

I just couldn't keep on top of it. Every surface became coated daily in a grey film, and outside was even worse. The saving grace was that all the houses were the same. The community pong came back with a vengeance and we were forced to unscrew the drain cover and give the sewerage pipes from the house a good swill down. It was not the most pleasant job to be doing in temperatures of 34 degrees. The smell lifted and we vowed to repeat the process every fortnight until the summer came to an end, or until we had a good downpour. Rain is a great sewer freshener and I hope to remember to give it more respect in the future. Tony began to spend increasing amounts of time inside as he was finding it difficult to breathe, especially when the wind dropped, and there were periods during the day when it was impossible to do anything much other than sit still or lie down. The intense heat of the sun was fading our clothes and the washing was drying so quickly that some items were fading dramatically whilst others seemed to be rotting. My peg basket shattered like a piece of brandy snap and the tiles around the pool were far too hot to walk on in bare feet.

It was a relief when a couple of weeks later I arrived back in Manchester to prepare for my interview. The UK floods had abated, the rain had cleared up, and I was greeted by a succession of crisp, bright days. Few people knew that I was back so I had plenty of time to myself to settle down, do some writing, and research the background of the firm to which I had applied. If they did not want me, it would not be because I had not tried.

The day of my interview finally arrived and, instead of feeling the same sort of excitement I had when I was notified about it, I felt totally sick with anxiety. I had diarrhoea, had hardly slept and felt like throwing up. My nerves were completely frazzled and I just didn't know what had brought it all on. In my head I didn't feel worried about it but for some reason my body was going to pieces. In the end, I rang Tony and suddenly it all came out. Exasperated, he said "But I thought you wanted this job" and I said that I did but that if I took it we would be apart for long periods again, only this time I would be in the UK and he would be in Spain. He said that we would work it out and I said that I just wanted us both to come back home and live a normal boring life. I couldn't see the point of the Spanish venture any longer, we weren't together enough to persevere with it and we never had been. Between stifled sobs, I told him that I would rather sell both properties, accept any losses and work hard to make it up. I could always earn more money but I couldn't replace the time we were spending apart. I missed him desperately and right at that moment I needed him with me like I had never needed him before and he just wasn't there. Finally, I pulled myself together and tried to focus on the interview; it was not a good day to be having a breakdown.

After 20 months of living in the sun I had very few smart clothes to my name but had managed to cobble together a reasonable outfit from a bag that had remained unopened since we had left. It would have to do. My next-door neighbour in Spain had given me an 'interview haircut' and I had found my old work shoes in a box under the bed. It felt strange to have them on rather than my usual sandals.

The interview was surprisingly informal and easygoing. I was told, unofficially, that I had been successful. The official confirmation would follow a couple of weeks later and then a start date would be arranged. I felt remarkably fortunate to be offered a job at my age at the first attempt and I hoped that getting back into the rat race would not prove to be too much for me. In my heart I was making my best effort to put right what I viewed as my error; feeling that it was all my responsibility, and I so desperately wanted to make things up to my loved ones and to feel better again.

I rang Tony to tell him the 'good news' and I started to feel a little more relaxed. I celebrated with a trip to Marks and Spencer's food hall and went home to indulge myself.

The next day I was confined to the flat with the 'runs'. The richness of the ready-meal and cream cake had caused havoc with my system and it had all gone straight though me. Clearly, my body had adapted to the healthier diet in Spain and it was not keen on this latest assault of fatty food. I was careful what I ate for the rest of my stay.

I remained in Manchester for a further two weeks and increasingly found myself at a loose end. Back in Spain, I would have gone for a walk or chatted to the neighbours, had a swim or sat outside to read or write. In Manchester, I watched TV. When the time finally came I headed back to Spain, and Tony, with enthusiasm, and felt the dread of emotional inconsistency washing over me yet again. When I was in Spain I wanted to be in Manchester, but when I was in Manchester I wanted to be in Spain – both emotions were equally strong and I really did not know what I was going to do about it.

What didn't help was the amount of time Tony and I were spending apart. It always seemed to me that I missed him more than he missed me, and that he genuinely *was* happy wherever he happened to have a bed for the night. That was probably why we never came to a concrete decision, and why I was in such turmoil – I just didn't know where we were heading. The lack of clarity wasn't fazing Tony one bit, but it had me in tatters.

The relief I felt when I landed back at Alicante airport was unbelievable and I am sure that for the most part it was because I was finally back in Tony's company. I was still convinced that the job was the answer to our short-term problems and that I would readjust to being back in the UK, given time.

September 2007 –
Janet In A New Crisis

September was a peaceful month for us. I was determined to enjoy my final weeks in Spain and the new arrangements left me feeling more relaxed. The official job offer came through and we agreed a start date of October 9th (two days after Tony's birthday). Apart from a couple of unexpected, but very spectacular thunderstorms, the weather remained pleasant and I swam almost every day. I felt stress-free and relaxed for the first time in ages. I think I even smiled occasionally. I shed no tears and slept soundly. It was a beautiful feeling and I hoped that it would continue forever.

Janet, back in Birmingham, was not sharing our calm. She had returned to work in the supermarket she had left in 2005 and had slotted back into the old routine fairly well, albeit without any enthusiasm, but she was plagued by money worries and her son was having problems at school. Mark was not sending any money home as he was covering the payments on their villa, which was still on the market. They were considering reducing the price even further to free up the small amount of money they still had left in it. The prospect of selling at the end of the year was remote; most of the holidaymakers had gone at the end of the school holidays and Pauline had told me that business was dead (the agents were having weeks on end with no customers and the reps were being laid off earlier than usual).

Janet's daughter had found a job in a sandwich shop and they were all in rented accommodation. The pressure on her must have been enormous and one evening she did what I had been dreading – she tried to kill herself with Paracetamol and whisky. Thank God that some friends discovered her in time, and she was rushed to hospital by ambulance to have her stomach pumped. Her liver suffered permanent damage and she was booked in for psychiatric treatment. This strong and capable woman had been reduced to an emotional wreck by an ill-fated move to Spain. She could see no other way out and so had made the worst, and hardest, decision of her life.

I rang her several times after she was released from hospital, and was pleased to hear that the antidepressants she had been prescribed were working. She was having counselling twice a week and was trying just to get through life one day at a time. The medication had numbed her and I could tell that she really didn't believe that the future held much hope for her. All her ambition had deserted her and she seemed to have accepted defeat. Occasionally she would say that she would still like to return to Spain but I hoped for her sake that it would never happen.

Her son's behaviour and performance at school continued to deteriorate. He was a confused little boy but his new teacher labelled him a 'thug'. His behaviour was bound to be bad, and more understanding would have gone a long way towards helping him. After all, he was taken out of his UK school to spend two years in a Spanish school, lost his dad and his dog and returned to the UK school at an educational level behind his peer group. I don't know how much he was consulted about the move, but he is undoubtedly one of the casualties of his parents' decision to emigrate. Your heart has to go out to the kid and it is anyone's guess how the problems he is storing up inside will manifest themselves later in life. Janet is doing her best to make things right for him, but there are days when she can barely function herself.

No one could ever claim that Janet, Mark, or their children have in any way lived a dream. The financial and emotional cost to the four of them has been phenomenal and I can fully understand why Janet really felt that she could not possibly go on. In stark contrast, back in Spain Tony and I were having a great time. Fiesta week was coming up at the beginning of October, and there was lots of talk about giant paellas, displays, the crowning of queens and other fun events.

Towards the end of September, we received the sad news that one of our neighbours had died. It was our first experience of death in Spain and it had several of us thinking about what we would do in a similar position. The Spanish seem to despatch their dead very swiftly and were prepared to cremate the chap involved the day after his death. His wife had to quickly arrange through a translator for a delay so that her children could get out for the funeral. We wondered what she would do; stay or go? I was certain that if anything ever happened to Tony that I would go straight back to the UK. Quite a few others felt the same but one or two said they would like to think they would give it a go on their own, or admitted that they could not afford to go back even if they wanted to.

The service was simple and respectful, and we were told that the chap's wife would be staying on for a while to see how she coped. Having been alone in Spain myself, I hoped that she would be OK. The villas are large for one person and, when the shutters are down at night, you can feel like you're the only person on the planet.

Spain is in a strange position considering the high numbers of elderly expats resident on its costas. Their presence distorts the natural age balance of the population and puts a strain on specific services. Charities for the elderly do operate in this part of Spain and they provide support for many expats who find themselves in difficulty or whose partners have died. Social care is thin on the ground here, and whilst the country provides discounted holidays and community centres for its own elderly residents, foreigners rarely use these facilities. It is expected that family members will take care of an old person's welfare, and increasing numbers of elderly Brits are finding themselves alone and isolated at a time of life when they are particularly vulnerable. Again we had never thought that far ahead, but I know that the charitable agencies are worried about the increasing numbers of such people now in this category, and it is difficult to know what to do for them. Many have lived in Spain for 10 or 20 years and yet still speak little or no Spanish. Often they end up in hospital and find themselves isolated by their lack of ability to communicate. I would hate to have someone talking over me about a medical condition, and not know what was going on. Yes, translators are provided, but they are not available on an individual basis and are not there to break up the day with a casual conversation. We should all think about such things and factor them into our plans.

October To December 2007

October arrived and I had only eight days left as a permanent fixture in Spain. I was looking forward to having some structure back in my life and earning an honest wage. Tony's 59th birthday was on the seventh and I was to start work on the ninth so a return to the UK on the eighth was cutting it fine, but we wanted to be together for as long as possible.

The town parade was to take place on his birthday and we had both signed up with the locals to join in the fun in fancy dress. About 40 of us dressed up as pirates and helped to hand out free beer to the crowd. We had a fabulous time and returned to the villa in the early hours of the morning on a complete high. It was the first time we had really felt involved in the town's events and it occurred to me that I was turning away from it just as we were about to be really accepted. I also felt a pang of irrational jealousy, knowing Tony would get to stay and enjoy the rest of fiesta week whilst I was remounting the same old treadmill back in England. Still, it had been my decision to look for a job and I had to face up to my responsibilities.

I bit back tears at Murcia airport; wishing that Tony would come with me to support me on my first day and also wishing that my fairy godmother would come down, wave a magic wand and make the world all right for me. I didn't know what had gone on in my head over the past couple of years to make me so childishly inconsistent but I just couldn't help it. Occasionally I would mentally tell myself to grow up and knuckle down, but minutes later I would be thinking about selling everything and running home to my dad.

The plane was delayed, and I barely got back to my flat in time to nip out and buy a pint of milk and a box of cereal before the shops shut. The water pressure on the hot water boiler had dropped and the thing would not light up so next I had to find a screwdriver to re-pressurise it before I could have a bath.

After a long soak, I went to bed and slept like a baby. I awoke refreshed, before the alarm sounded, and set off for work feeling relaxed and confident. I truly believed that things were finally working out and that within 12 months we would be back on an even keel once more. Then the problems started. The tram was packed and I just managed to get on it, then it broke down and we were stuck between stations for 25 minutes. I eventually got off at St. Peter's Square and ran like an old fat maniac, across Manchester to Blackfriars Bridge where my new workplace was situated. I arrived with only one minute to spare; red and sweating like a pig. My calm had deserted me and I wanted to tell the receptionist that I had made a terrible mistake, get out of there and keep on running. I stayed.

My new boss was very young, but he was also very nice and started indoctrinating me into the company immediately. I had been told that four of us would be starting together but, for some reason, the other three had not turned up. I was on my own and being bombarded with information from the very first minute; put your name on your sandwiches or they will go in the bin, don't eat at your desk, don't leave the front door open, don't leave valuables in your coat….'Oh no!' I thought. This is not funny. This is not going to be good. Hang on; it will get better, surely? The rest of the first day consisted of a tour, a lecture on quality, a lecture on health and safety, a lecture on company policy, sickness, overtime, lateness, breaks; on and on and on it went. Noooooooooo!!!! My brain was shouting 'information overload, get out, get out!' I stayed.

At the end of the day, totally exhausted, I rejoined the anonymous throng heading back towards the tram. There was a strange whistling sound in my head, a man was asleep in a flowerbed, another asked me for money, a free newspaper was thrust into my hand, and I bought a *Big Issue*. On Cross Street, I saw a Unitarian church. It must have been there for years but I had never noticed it before. It looked like a place of refuge but unfortunately it wasn't because it was locked. I don't really know what Unitarians are but at that moment I really wanted to go in there and find some inner peace; it was not to be. The noise, buildings, and crowds of Manchester were closing in on me, and I was unnerved by it all. The feeling came as a shock, it was completely unexpected and I wasn't sure what to make of it.

Back in the flat, I didn't feel hungry and had a bowl of cereal for my evening meal. It failed to make me feel any better. I told Tony, my dad and my brother that the day had been a tiring one and I was full of information, but that I was sure it would improve once I actually started to do some work. I slept well again and the following day's tram journey was smooth and uneventful.

On day two, I was brainwashed with corporate information – history, turnovers, mergers, amalgamations, figures, share prices, and company scandals. I was seated in front of a computer and left to work my way through a 'corporatise yourself' programme whilst the manager got on with something more important. It was modular brainwashing – I steadily worked my way through the stages completing the tests along the way and awarded myself a certificate eight hours later that declared that I could '*Think Blue*'. I was locked in my own little world and no one spoke to me – it was a 'no talking' department. No one went on their break with anyone else either as the desks had to be manned at all times – one chap whispered to me that he had been there two years and still did not know half the people in the room. A woman I met in the toilets told me I was mad to swap Spain for such a job – she hated it and would have swapped with me any day of the week. I could see that she thought that the Spanish opportunity had been wasted on someone like me and that someone like her would have made a better go of it. She was probably right.

At lunchtime, I went to see if the Unitarians were up to anything and I managed to sit in on a service. I didn't know if I should be in there really – I am Church of England but I don't know what sort. It was the first time in my life that I had set foot into a church for a service and I found the experience quite calming but also quite emotional. The speaker (he didn't look like a priest) had a lot to say but the only words I heard were 'one hour's misery wipes out all memory of delight'. I think he was quoting from the Bible and I felt that he was talking directly to me; I had found myself at a new low spot in my life and I could not remember any joy in it. The man seemed to be looking directly at me – he seemed to know that I wanted someone to take me somewhere safe and sort out my mess for me – and I knew it was not going to happen. Perhaps I looked manic or just desperate, I really do not know, but I wanted to stay and have tea and a chat with this man and I knew that I couldn't because I had to get back to work. I detested the way that the pull of the clock had so quickly imposed itself once again upon my life and I wanted to rage against it. I left quickly at the end of the service and returned to my new prison.

With hindsight now I believe that I was on the verge of falling into depression and I was using up my energy fighting it – leaving nothing in reserve to concentrate on the new job or the adjustment back to city living. I had been back only two days and I was sinking fast. 'Here we go again', I thought, "Tony and me stuck in different places – Tony largely happy with his lot and me going round the twist'. All my strategies to correct my mistakes were failing, and the 'just give it time and don't mess about with it' approach was taking far too long. I had a restless night.

I hoped that day three would be lighter and more related to what I would be doing, but my hopes were dashed when I was informed that I would have to sit through a 'product day', which was not very relevant to me, but I had to go to it because they had nowhere else to put me. I went along and listened to pitches from suppliers of goods I would never use. The whole thing lasted eight hours with only two ten-minute breaks – my brain had had enough.

The tram journey home passed in a blur and as soon as it reached my stop, I rushed back to the flat and breathed a massive sigh of relief as I slammed my own front door firmly shut. I went to bed early to regain some strength, but I awoke at about 3am with an unpleasant tingling sensation running up and down my body – I was panicking in my sleep. Deep within me I knew that I was about to let everybody down once again. I spent the rest of the night tossing and turning; just aching for someone to talk to. No matter how old you are, there are times in your life when you just want your parents. Unfortunately, the person I really wanted to talk to was my mum, who had been dead since 1995, so I tried to think my way out of the problem instead. (Tony hates it when I think).

At 7am, I switched on my computer and e-mailed my new boss my resignation. I confessed that I would not stick with his company long enough to justify the expense of training me and thanked him for the opportunity – he thanked me for my honesty and we officially parted company. The truth was that I hated the crowds of the city and the job had been too much like the one I had left behind. I had been out of the rat race in a sleepy Spanish village for two years and the pace of life in Manchester now scared me. I simply couldn't stomach the corporate bullshit any more; I needed a more sedate occupation and time to get my head together. My failure also meant that I was back to a position of having no income. I changed tactics and began to consider shelf stacking in the local supermarket as an occupation that would suit my current state of mind. My history teacher at school told me that Winston Churchill had said, "When you are going through hell you should just keep going". I took it to mean that eventually you would come out at the other side and find yourself in a better place. It sounded like good advice, but I wasn't sure where my resolve was going to come from.

Another marathon thinking session led to the sudden decision to put the Manchester flat back up for sale. It is beautiful but at the end of the day, it is only bricks and mortar. It had always been our plan to sell it and we had kept it on only because of Tony's collapse, my dad's unease and latterly my need for a UK bolthole. The standing charges were draining our finances, and my extreme reaction to the job and the environment had made me believe that I would not be able to live and work in Manchester on a permanent basis ever again. Geographically it no longer served a purpose for us. Tony is from South Wales and I am from West Yorkshire. It seemed silly to me for us to have most of our money tied up in a property we were hardly using, and which was not close to either of our families. We had only ever lived in Manchester because of our lines of work. I reasoned that they would need shelf stackers in West Yorkshire and that when we came back from Spain I might possibly prefer to live closer to my dad and my brother.

No longer able to trust my own judgement I ran the idea past Tony and my dad, and both thought it was the right thing to do, so I wasted no time and called an estate agent in. The flat was on the market within 48 hours and I hoped that the agent's sales pitch, which stated that they aimed to achieve an acceptable offer within eight weeks, would turn out to be true. The way the apartment in Spain was performing, I wasn't expecting an acceptable offer in my lifetime!

I expected to be able to relax once a firm strategy had been agreed upon but, within me, there was a residual disappointment that I had not been able to cope with the UK pace of life. It took several, emotionally difficult, days for those feelings to pass and I tried to channel my energy into rounding off the book and looking for a publisher.

I returned to Spain a couple of weeks later to collect a few things and said my goodbyes to friends for the time being, which was just as well because Tony had his most spectacular blackout only days after I got back. We now refer to it as his 'Del Boy blackout' because it involved him disappearing through the gap in a bar. It was the same bar in Los Altos where he had had his first incident, so they knew he had a tendency to want to take a closer look at the floor tiles. We heard a bang and the owner shouted me. Tony had gone through the gap, nutted the fridge at the back of the bar and broken his ribs on a hard object on the way down. As usual, he came round after about 30 seconds. He had a huge lump on his head and was incredibly embarrassed as the bar was quite full. He was badly shaken, and chose to recover his composure by lighting up a fag; the fags had caused the condition in the first place. In true British style we tried to laugh the incident off by saying things like, "Who the bloody hell do you think you are, David Jason?" and "That's one way of getting out of buying a round." It took him longer to recover from this particular incident simply because his ribs took weeks to heal. I was on edge hoping that he didn't have another blackout in quick succession as they could have done some serious internal damage if they took a second knock. A course of steroids sorted him out and we relaxed once more. In late November, we returned to the UK for Christmas.

Christmas was a frugal affair, but we enjoyed it nonetheless. The first draft of the book was rejected, albeit with some positive criticism, and I utilised my free time making adjustments. We also decided to put the villa onto the market and try to sell any or all of the properties for a completely fresh start. Then Tony persuaded me to give Spain another six months and to concentrate on finding work there in the hope that we would shift a property when the new tourist season began at the end of March. We booked flights for January 3rd 2008 and Tony uttered those dreaded words "2008 is going to be our year." He just can't help himself.

January To March 2008 –
It's A Buyer's Market

The first quarter of 2008 flew by and was not too bad for us personally because we were busy. I applied for several jobs without success, but I also decided to apply to be a volunteer for local charity supporting the elderly as a 'home visitor'. They accepted me following a vetting process, and I spent a few weeks helping out at their social centre whilst waiting to be allocated an elderly person who wanted someone to visit them in their home. At the centre I met a woman who told me that she and her husband had tried to move back to the UK six times and had returned to Spain within a couple of months each time. She said the place and the pace of life somehow got a grip of you and you could not shake it off as easily as you thought. She settled my mind – I appreciated that I was not alone and that my indecision and inconsistency were not peculiar to me. Lots of the volunteers seemed to have been through similar doubts to mine and, like me, had taken up voluntary work to inject some purpose back into their lives. Such organisations provide a vital support network for the elderly, infirm and lonely, and volunteers are always in short supply.

On the property front, I sacked Janet's agent who was handling the non-sale of the apartment, and put the villa onto the market with a Spanish agent in Los Montesinos. The appearance of the 'Se Vende' sign inevitably stirred the interest of the neighbours who wanted to know why we were selling and how much we were asking. We kept the story brief and told people that urbanisation living was not suiting us and that we were looking elsewhere. We tried to remain upbeat about the prospect of selling *something* but it was clear that the sub-prime mortgage fiasco in the USA was having a worldwide impact. Additionally, the pound was beginning to struggle against the euro; all the expats we knew were complaining about the exchange rate, and the number of euros they were losing compared with the same period in 2007. This was to be a recurring theme for the months ahead, with some hit far harder than others. One friend reported that he knew of a woman who had taken a job paying only €2.50 per hour for a 12-hour shift in a pub kitchen to top up her depleted pension. That is €30 (or about £23 at the time), for 12 hours of illegal work. Can anyone tell me how this equates to 'living a dream'? Or am I *really* missing the point of it all?

Towards the end of March, Pauline and Phil from the property company made contact with us and reported that their son had closed down his small business and had returned to the UK to find less precarious work. Pauline was clearly upset, as she had only agreed to live in Spain if their son came too. By this time, they had been here for seven years and I thought they would be permanent fixtures, but that scenario no longer looked certain. Pauline's work was also becoming patchy. The property company she worked for had cut down the number of reps from 64 to 14 and the other co-ordinators had been dismissed. Pauline feared that the workforce was becoming so small that it would be absorbed into the much larger parent company, and that they would effectively cease to exist as a separate entity. In the meantime, she was accepting all the work that they could provide her with and she had been forced to go to the bank to discuss her future ability to pay the mortgage on her rural property, which had still not sold. Her finca had been on the market since 2004 and had had only four viewings. Her bank manager was sympathetic but not particularly helpful; an extension to the life of the mortgage, to reduce the monthly repayments, was all that was on offer, and that came with an 'arrangement fee' of €1000, which could not be added to the loan. Like the banks in the UK, Spanish banks were becoming nervous of lending money on property, and mortgages in general were becoming harder to secure. Pauline had done the sensible thing and approached her bank before any real trouble arose; too many were ignoring the problem until they were about to fall into arrears. Rumour had it that if you missed six payments the bank would automatically repossess the property and sell it at auction. Some banks were even accused of not publicising sales and buying up the properties themselves at prices that just covered the mortgages, leaving nothing in reserve to be paid to the now homeless evictees. An increasing number of individuals were simply choosing to throw their house keys back to the banks and walk away from the mess.

I looked into the option of selling at auction and decided to give it a go with the apartment. The main benefit I could foresee was that if it attracted a successful bid, the buyer would have to pay in full within 28 days. The downside was that we would have to price the property at a level that would attract viewers and bids. The auctioneers were very efficient and we did achieve some viewings, which gave us renewed hope. I paid €178 to list the property in the auction catalogue and the sale fee would be 3% if it sold. We went to watch, full of hope. It did not attract one bid. We were disappointed with the lack of a sale but satisfied with the service and the efforts of the auctioneers. A couple of weeks later I received a letter from them offering to put the apartment into the next auction free of charge. Of course, I accepted. No opportunity could be sniffed at.

The auction option had become particularly tempting because auctions attracted serious buyers with the cash available to complete the sale within four weeks. Via the more conventional route, Janet and Mark had accepted an offer from a UK 'buyer' in October 2007; eight months later, they had still not completed. Their old family home had been off the market and standing empty for eight months whilst they waited for money from someone who could not complete because he had not sold his own property in the UK. At the same time, the fluctuation in the exchange rate was increasing the final cost to their purchaser, making the chances of him pulling out of the deal, or reducing his offer, highly likely. Janet was tearing her hair out back in Birmingham; her life could not move forwards without her share of the money. Mark was struggling to pay for the property in the interim period and the electricity had been cut off. The 'buyers' deposit was being used to pay the mortgage, eating into the sum available for them to divide at the end of the process, if it ever came.

Back in our own villa, the viewers were spouting the 'it's a buyer's market', line and irritating us. We found that if we asked the right questions, very few were buyers at all, but were actually sellers themselves with no pot of cash. They were in no position to negotiate and we would not deal with them. One couple were genuinely in love with the villa and wanted it, but we refused their suggestion to pay us a small sum to take it off the market whilst they sorted out their own sale. This is what Janet and Mark had done and it had trapped them into a deal without any clear end date. (This is a wake up call to all those viewers fond of trotting out the 'buyer's market' line. HELLO! You are <u>not a buyer</u> if you haven't got any money, so kindly keep the smug sound bites to yourself.)

To be fair to our Los Montesinos agent he was doing his best to drum up genuine customers; we had more viewings at the villa in two weeks than we had had at the apartment in a year. I felt certain that the villa would go – eventually.

In the UK, our Manchester flat was attracting little attention and what the agent termed 'feedback' was actually getting my back up. "The client doesn't like the view"; "There is no lift"; "The third bedroom is too small." Well thanks for that, but what could I do about it, so why tell me? I would rather simply have been told that the client was just not interested. If the agent had said that the colours of the walls were putting people off I would have happily repainted, but there was sod all I could do about the view, or the size of the third bloody bedroom!

In February, I contacted a Costa Blanca based publisher and submitted a 20000-word sample of my amended manuscript. I was delighted to be contacted a few weeks later with a request for the rest. My hopes were up again. Tony and I decided that we would personally deliver the two full copies requested rather than risk putting them into the Spanish postal system. Armed with maps we set off in search of a place called Benimaurell with instructions to leave the manuscripts behind the bar of the local hostelry. Tony and I never reach our destinations at the first attempt, and we stopped off in a small town close to Benimaurell to ask for directions, as the signs to it had run out. In a bar, several customers crowded around my inadequate map and argued amongst themselves as to which direction we should take. As the locals were voting for *all* the directions out of town, I began to suspect that none of them really knew where Benimaurell was. Eventually an English chap said, very positively, "Go towards Flesh and past the lunatic asylum, it's at the top of the mountain." The map-readers all suddenly remembered that this was definitely the way and I rejoined Tony in the car. As I passed on the directions, he repeated the words 'Flesh' and 'lunatic asylum' in a strained, increasingly high-pitched, tone. It was beginning to sound like a dangerous outing. For once, we were completely united on something, and considered doing a runner back to Los Montesinos and using the 'iffy' postal system after all. Fleix turned out to be a small hamlet on the way to our destination, which was indeed at the top of a mountain – the car was so vertical I thought we were in an Apollo space rocket. I marvelled at how anyone could find a place like it, never mind decide that it was the ideal place to live. Benimaurell was closed for the siesta – not a soul was in sight – but we found the pub with no difficulty and the barman failed to bat an eyelid when I asked for two beers and "also can I leave this dodgy-looking package behind the bar." It could only happen in Spain.

The system worked and, four weeks later, we celebrated the news that the book had been accepted for publication. We hoped it signalled the turning point for our fortunes. Tony had to be calmed down and told that, no, he could not have a yacht because I was not going to be as rich as J.K.Rowling.

April To June 2008 –
Paid Work At Last

Our good fortune continued into the second quarter of the year. I had another interview, in Spanish, at one of the local electrical shops and, though I did not get the job, I was pleased with the improvement in my spoken Spanish since the Buddha-woman experience in 2006. My confidence rose and I eventually gained employment as a data-input clerk for an Internet-based company. The great thing was I could work from home; they e-mailed my work to me, along with a deadline; how I organised myself was entirely up to me.

We also received a bizarre offer for the Spanish apartment, which I had to turn down because I suspected the individual concerned of being involved in a money-laundering racket. In my e-mail inbox one morning, I had a communication from a 'doctor' offering to pay the full amount immediately for the apartment. This chap had not viewed the property, and after a little bit of research using the dialling code from his telephone number I discovered that he was based in Nigeria. I e-mailed him back, politely suggesting that he provide me with his solicitor's details, and offering to provide him with mine. The reply was that he would just like to pay me directly for it, in full, and that he would cover all the taxes and fees. Thank you, I replied, but this is not how we sell property in Spain (actually nobody is selling anything much in Spain at the moment). You have to have an NIE number, do all sorts of pesky legal stuff and have someone attend the notary's office for the transfer of the deeds. He said, 'Just let me have your bank account number and I will send you lots of money'. Somewhat reluctantly, I bid him goodbye. Just my luck! The only offer I'd had for the apartment had to be bloody illegal. I could understand why people would be tempted, but I didn't want to end up starring on 'Banged Up Abroad'. I reported my experience to Pauline and she said her company was selling to Nigerians, but only after they had gone through a lengthy military security check. For this reason, they were only selling them off-plan properties because quick sales were not possible.

Mid-April arrived, and so did Janet. This was her first visit since she had left the previous year, and she was nervous about seeing Mark again. They had to get together to sort out the issue of the villa, their marriage and child maintenance. The sale of their villa was still far from completed; they were going for weeks without any contact from their 'buyer' and Mark (who now had a contract for his welding work) was under serious financial pressure. The lack of electricity at the villa had the unfortunate side effect of a green, very unhealthy-looking pool, as the pump was out of operation, and the water was not circulating. They effectively had a stagnant pond at the front of the property. I worried that if their buyer returned for another look, the obvious lack of maintenance would put him off and he would use it as an excuse to back out of the deal. I urged Janet to go to the bank with Mark to explain the whole situation. The deposit money would not last forever and there was still no end in sight. Unfortunately, they did not go to the bank and allowed the matter to remain unresolved. Their reconciliation, however, was rather more successful than anyone imagined it would be and there were signs that they might rekindle their relationship, despite the fact that Mark was still shacked up with 'the other woman'. Isn't life complicated? Consequently, we did not see much of her during her stay, and I deposited her back at Murcia airport, under the influence of Jack Daniels, seven days later wearing an outfit of her mother's as she had been sick down her own skirt. Lovely!

Towards the end of April, the local free papers were publicising a new 'reality' TV show called *No Place Like Home* and were asking for interested parties to volunteer to appear. The show would apparently offer homesick, or otherwise desperate, expats the chance to test-drive a return to life in the UK. Possibly great entertainment if you are not involved, but not very funny if you are. Coincidentally, in May, another channel began to televise a series called *House Trapped In The Sun*. To me it was confirmation that the dream-selling process had definitely run its course. One presenter was happily flogging foreign properties to us five or six years ago, now she was trying to look concerned as people told her of the nightmares they had found themselves in. Frankly, I thought it a bit rich that she should get to keep her career running off the back of it all. The *No Place Like Home* article reported that over 100,000 Brits went back to the UK from 'dream lives' abroad in 2007. How can so many people get it so wrong? We are either all crackers or there is something seriously amiss with the process.

Work was a great tonic and, though the pay was not fantastic, we at least had regular money topping up Tony's pension and our savings were being preserved for real emergencies and not being eroded by daily expenses. The middle of May brought with it an approach from a cash buyer for the villa, and we began a slow bartering process. Luckily, the chap already lived not far from us in Spain so it felt far more normal than the long distance situation that Janet and Mark had found themselves caught up in. I tried not to get my hopes up, but prayed for the day that we would come to an amicable agreement. I did not want to lose the 'buyer' because he claimed to be genuinely in a position to buy quickly. Ideally, we wanted the villa off our hands by the end of July as all the notaries traditionally took August off. No completion by the end of July would see the process drift into September and we would then be caught up in a backlog of paperwork. I contacted my currency broker to warn him of the possibility of my transferring a large sum back to the UK. For once things were in my favour financially and I could make money back as I turned euros into pounds.

The weather was uncharacteristically bad throughout May and the chances of a good swim in the pool were not high, as the water temperature was stubbornly refusing to increase. We had high winds and a fair amount of rain. That, combined with the poor exchange rate *and* the credit crunch, meant that very few tourists appeared for the half-term holidays and lots of bar owners started to worry about their businesses. Some began to lay off staff and in general, unemployment was on the increase. Many bars depend on the profits made in summer to keep going throughout the winter. A poor summer would be disastrous and some would close down before the end of the year. Rain was causing a recurring problem to raise its head yet again and the residents of La Zenia made the papers for the umpteenth time as raw sewage glided down their streets as the drains failed to cope. (The human waste apparently ends up on the beach, which is not a detail publicised in any brochure!)

The poor weather was keeping many of us indoors longer than we would have liked so it was unfortunate that at the same time many of us began to have problems receiving certain television stations. Our provider was in dispute with Sky, and a Spanish TV company, over the rebroadcast of certain channels, including Sky Sports. This caused lots of men to get their knickers in a twist over the reception of football (Tony was also disconnected from Homer Simpson and Adolf Hitler, much to my relief). We received free TV for a month as compensation, which I thought at the time was quite fair. I am sure that many people would not move to the costas if they could not watch their regular programmes and *The Big Match*. There is no doubt that it was potentially a big problem. When combined with the poor exchange rate, the downturn in the property market, the lack of tourists, and a drop in the wholesale price of lemons, Spain was having a hard time. The last thing it needed was thousands of people heading home because they could not keep up with *Eastenders*.

Pauline was now keeping in regular contact with us and hinted that we might want to consider a property swap. In better times, it might have been an attractive proposal, but much as I genuinely loved her finca, I could not consider isolating us in the mountains as we still had Mr Cash Buyer on the agenda. She then called round one day to say she knew someone 'off the books', who might want to buy our villa and who was going to be in Spain at the beginning of June. The catch was that the woman had two shops and a house to sell in the UK, and Pauline wanted me to bung her 3% commission if the sale went through. It was clearly a non-starter, and we were surprised that a friend would ask to be paid commission. The request was totally out of character and, as a sale was unlikely, we decided to forget it. Later, the reasons for her actions became much clearer to us, and the matter passed without incident.

In the middle of May, a coordinator from the charity contacted me with the details of a new client and we went off to meet the person concerned and do an assessment. The woman's son had requested help because his mother had started to become forgetful and was vulnerable to being ripped off. He told us that Maisie had lived in Spain for over 20 years and had coped marvellously with the loss of her husband and various health issues of her own, but someone offering 'companionship' had recently taken advantage of her. After gaining her confidence, the 'companion' had set about raiding her bank account and subsequently her utilities were disconnected owing to lack of funds. At the age of 82, she was unable to sort out the mess for herself, had lost confidence, and was reluctant to go out. Her son dealt with the disconnection problems and restricted her access to money so that she could not become a target for a second time. Her situation got me thinking once again about the difficulties of old age in a foreign country; it is a real problem, and one that hardly anyone plans for. I began visiting her on a weekly basis, taking her for a drink and having a chat about current affairs. She was a real character and had led a 'colourful' life; the TV was her contact with home, and the outside world, for the majority of the week, and she had opinions on everything from pole dancing to international terrorism. At the time, I think we were therapy for each other.

In June, Janet revealed, in one of our regular long distance phone calls, that she had given Mark an ultimatum about their marriage in the hope that he would give it one last chance. I didn't know where she thought 'the other woman' would fit into the scheme as he was still living with her, but you can't knock Janet's optimism. I doubted that Mark would respond well to the ultimatum and felt that she would be left feeling rejected all over again. I also thought that dragging her son back to Spain after a year in a UK school would be unwise, but she seemed to think it might be a good idea, and it really was none of my business how she chose to live her life. I suspected that during her week in Spain during April,

Mark had given her false hope during a drinking session and she had taken it as a sign that reconciliation really was on the cards. Janet would be the first to admit that she was finding it difficult to stop loving him. She would not have split from him, had he not been having the affair, and given a push, at the time, she probably would have had him back (even though she replaced his name with the title 'Nobhead' on her mobile phone, so that it flashed up every time he rang her). Sensibly, she had not expressed these emotions in front of her son. She said she would let me know what happened. I updated her on the state of the pool at their villa, which by now looked like green jelly, was attracting mosquitoes, and giving off an unpleasant cabbagey/bad egg aroma. She just laughed; it was the least of her problems.

At the end of the month we spoke again and she informed me that Mark's response to her ultimatum was that getting back together was 'A bit difficult at the moment' (in other words 'No'). Apparently, he had been arrested, and had his car, passport and driving licence confiscated by the Guardia Civil (we both agreed this *was* a bit of a barrier to free travel). Additionally the house he was renting with 'the other woman' was being repossessed, and they had been given a couple of weeks to vacate the premises. What I didn't tell Janet, in the light of all she was telling me, was that a rumour had started on our urbanisation that her own villa was in the process of being repossessed. I wasn't sure it was true; she clearly hadn't heard anything, and I didn't want to worry her even more. On top of that, some of the residents nearest to their pool, which, by now, was clearly a stinking health hazard and mosquito nightclub, wanted to take out a denuncia against them to force them to clean it up (with no electricity this was going to be difficult anyway, otherwise I think Mark would have done it). All in all, it was turning into a bit of a bugger.

As the weather finally began to behave and be more Spanish than English, our pool became usable at last and I restarted a long abandoned keep-fit campaign. That, coupled with a steady trickle of work, my visits to Maisie, and rounding off the book for the publisher, kept me occupied, and my spirits up.

In the middle of June, Pauline's unofficial 'customer' arrived and was clearly not interested in buying anything; very sensibly, she was looking for a long-term let whilst she had a good look around. She had the three properties to sell back in the UK and, going on my experience, I didn't fancy her chances. Anyway, the woman was in no rush and I completely discounted her (with some relief, as it meant that my friendship with Pauline would not be put under any strain by the 3% issue). Pauline had been right in one respect – the woman was an ideal person for the villa, it was just what she was looking for and she loved it – if only she had any money. At last, it became clear why Pauline had gone to the extreme of asking us for a percentage; she confessed that she had lost her job; and with it her car and mobile phone. Her company was running on a skeleton staff, completing only those transactions that were already in the system. No customers, no sales, no money, no jobs just about summed up the situation. That was now two of the 'big boys' down the road; things really were getting worse.

The demise of two big agents did not raise any sympathy amongst the expat population locally; most of us felt disgruntled with them over something, and we all felt that they had been too greedy and had contributed to the problem by keeping prices and commissions high when the market was clearly failing. The attitude of most people was 'serves them right'.

Meanwhile my agent back in Manchester was beginning to annoy me with his meaningless feedback, requests for price reductions and lack of action. Then he sent me a letter asking if I would like to put my property into his latest fantastic scheme – a 'property sale'. I e-mailed him back saying, "Isn't that what you are supposed to do anyway; sell property? Isn't that the point of an estate agent or am I missing the trick here?" He didn't reply.

By the end of June, after a long drawn out negotiation, we realised that Mr Cash Buyer was a fraud and had suddenly become un-contactable. Getting the price down had been a game to him; he had had his fun and slithered off. In Spain, an Englishman's word is apparently worth nothing until the cash is in the bank. We went through the same problems a second time before we eventually sold to a decent couple that stuck to exactly what had been agreed.

July To September 2008 –
TV Or No TV
That Is The Question

By July the television situation had settled down again; we had a different combination of channels, but we could still receive BBC and ITV. Rumours abounded about the future of British TV reception in Spain, but as there was little we could do about it, there was no point in getting worked up. I was looking forward to the Olympic Games, and just hoped that transmission would continue until they ended. The pound continued to struggle against the euro; one or two people were feeling the pinch financially and began grumbling about life in Spain not being as cheap as it used to be and a few packed up and went home. But all in all things were going well; I was shortlisted for a job in a bookshop and my weekly visits to Maisie, were proving to be a real tonic. She could be a bit repetitive but was in possession of all her marbles and she told some great stories about her past. It was nice to be doing something for someone else. Generally, my mood was good, the sun was shining, and the weeks were flying by. We accepted another phantom offer on the villa from a couple that had to nip home and sort out the transfer of their money; they never came back. Luckily, after our Mr Cash Buyer experience, I had quickly sensed that they were scoring high on the 'idiot scale' so I wasn't surprised when they disappeared.

The beginning of August brought with it the start of the Olympics and I settled down to two weeks of viewing. Two days later the British channels began to become unreliable again and by day four, those of us with 'mesh' aerials were disconnected. Tony managed to reconnect the communal Spanish aerial and I was able to watch some events without fully understanding the commentary. The local press kept us up to date with the 'will we ever be reconnected' gossip, but it became clear that it was not going to happen when the Guardia Civil dismantled the main transmission antenna of the company that we paid for our signal. Some smaller companies were still able to transmit a limited range of programmes but the police ordered them to cease broadcasting Sky channels. Bars with systems set up for *The Big Match Live* quickly had to find alternative sources; those that didn't lost a lot of custom to those that did.

Some of our neighbours quickly bought systems from alternative providers, but with the villa on the market, I was unwilling to spend any more money on it. Tony and I decided to give it a few weeks to see what happened. Luckily, we are both avid readers so the prospect of no television was inconvenient but not devastating. The letter pages of the *Costa Blanca News*, and bar conversations, were dominated by those expressing differing viewpoints on the situation. The ones I found the most insensitive were those who smarmily declared that we would 'all have to start getting out more and talking to each other rather than watching the box'. Well that's fine if you *can* get out or if you *have* someone to talk to. Maisie was beginning to struggle without the stimulation of news programmes and her favourite soaps. During the first four weeks without TV, I noticed her mental state begin to deteriorate, the sparkle went out of her conversation, and she began to look grey and sad. Her son tried his best to get her an alternative but she was in a bit of a transmission black-spot and her ancient system was not suitable for a cheap, quick retune. The eventual effect on her was to prove to be devastating.

At the beginning of September, my Spanish estate agent rang to say he had customers who wanted to view the villa. As usual, he wanted to come around immediately so we raced around the house quickly tidying up and putting things away. Half an hour later I was seated in his office signing a contract and being given a cash deposit to put in my handbag. The only downside to the transaction was that he had thrown in all my furniture without consulting me first, but I just thought 'sod it', and accepted the deal. He arranged a notary date for the middle of October, and the buyer went back to the UK to sort the money out. It looked like we were finally moving!

Back in the UK Janet had found herself a lovely new boyfriend and was getting back into the swing of life. It was great to hear the change in her voice; she was upbeat, about to become a grandmother for the second time, and much more like her old carefree self. She was getting over Mark and it was doing her the world of good; the repossession of their villa had gone ahead and she really couldn't care less.

Pauline also had some good news. She and Phil had accepted an offer for their mountain retreat. We could be moving at the same time. Things were looking up for all of us. It felt great; we were all coming out of the gloom together.

Maisie's mindset however, continued to go downhill and she became increasingly confused. She craved the company of the television, and was spending long lonely days sitting on the sofa staring into space. The apartments on her row were vacated at the end of the school holidays, and around her there was only silence – no sound of human life from anywhere. It would have driven me crazy, and I could get out under my own steam. Towards the end of September, she began to drive her family crackers with bizarre phone calls, and she became increasingly forgetful and rather belligerent and awkward like a difficult child. I reported the change in her demeanour to my boss and her family was contacted to discuss her long-term ability to continue living alone.

October To December 2008 –
On The Move

My appointment with the notary to officially hand over the villa to its new owners was set for the middle of October. Everything continued to progress according to plan. I obtained several documents to ensure the appointment went as smoothly as possible, including the latest copies of bills, receipts for my local taxes and a certificate from the community administrators to prove that I had not defaulted on my community fees. Debt tends to remain with a property, rather than with an individual, in Spain so buyers should take steps to ensure that no amounts are left outstanding or they are likely to inherit them along with their new dream home. A Spanish friend arranged an appointment for me with his solicitor and I was pleasantly surprised to discover that the solicitor could claim up to €7500 back for me in overpaid taxes once the transaction had been completed at the land registry. It was either something to do with the price we had accepted for the villa, or that I was a non-resident, but had I not gone to the solicitor I would never have known. I wondered how many Brits had not had this information simply because they decided to chance it and go without legal representation. The solicitor said it could take six to twelve months for the refund to come through, so I'm sure many people must go home without making a claim. Anyway, he was quite right, and €6850 appeared in my bank account eleven months after I had sold the villa.

Tony made one of his trips home to check on his mum, whilst I boxed up and transported our personal effects to the apartment. By now, I was relieved that my estate agent had included the furniture; it saved a lot of hassle and meant we could have a real fresh start back in Los Altos. I borrowed inflatable beds from friends, and we were sorted. Pauline's sale was also still progressing, but their buyer had asked for an extra month to complete, as his dog's pet passport prevented the animal from travelling until November. Understandably, this made her a bit nervous, but we all kept making positive comments to stop her nerves from becoming completely frazzled.

My buyer returned from the UK as promised and, at last, the day of my notary appointment arrived. My agent took us all off in his people carrier and, on arrival, we went straight through to the notary's office. It looked like things were going to get done quickly. It was not to be. The process took four and a half hours! The notary examined my bills and paperwork in the finest detail. I sat there feeling sick, praying that I had not overlooked anything and that the buyer would not be scared off if he refused to complete the sale that day because of some minor detail. He pulled a lot of faces, had the contract retyped twice and wasn't happy with the receipt I had produced for my local taxes, so he went for a lengthy break whilst his secretary had a copy of my payments faxed over from the tax office. Eventually he came back in and the translator said, "You don't owe anything." He finally signed the papers, I handed over the keys, and we were out of there. Phew! I paid my agent his fee in cash and he wrote out an unofficial-looking receipt, whilst promising to change over the electricity and water contracts into the new owner's name the following week (unlike in the UK nobody read the meters on the day of moving). He was good to his word, but I had to wait a month for the final utility bill payments to debited from my account.

In the meantime, Tony and I became avid monitors of the exchange rate so that we could cash in on the weakness of the pound against the euro. Ironically, even though I had sold the villa for less than I had paid for it in euros, I was guaranteed a profit if I repatriated the money to the UK. It was not such a bad time to be selling after all.

By late November, Pauline's buyers arrived with their dog and her sale went through. Like me, she had a heart-stopping moment when the notary pointed out that the outbuildings of the property did not appear on the land registry's paperwork. Pauline and Phil had to instantly agree to hand over €4000 to correct the error before the official would sign the sale off. It's a good job they didn't hesitate. Pauline and Phil went off to celebrate and within a couple of hours the new owners were on the phone complaining that the TV (which they themselves had had installed prior to moving in) did not work. Phil patiently talked them through the process of what to press and promptly forgot about them. Four days later Pauline took a call from the female of the couple. She was crying, she hated the property, it was in the middle of nowhere, there were no English people around, and she wanted to go home. Pauline said "Give it a chance, you've only been here four days; we had seven wonderful years in that house", "Well in that case you can buy it back, or rent it off us," snapped the woman.

The call upset Pauline; she is a sensitive person, and she felt responsible even though she obviously was not. The woman had robbed her of the joy of achieving the sale and the accompanying reduction in stress that she had been looking forward to. Phil, Tony, and I told her not to take any more calls. Pauline had not deceived the couple in any way; they had viewed the property twice and had stayed for many hours each time. They knew it was in the middle of nowhere – they had driven to it for goodness sake, and if they had not checked out the local amenities, it was hardly Pauline's fault. They had also been given a big reduction off the asking price; what more did they want? Still Pauline fretted. Eventually she spoke to the agent who had sold the property for them and he told her that after only three days under new ownership, it had been put back onto the market and the couple in question were in the process of packing up and going home. Now that *must* be a record!

Back in Los Altos, Tony and I were relaxed and adjusting to life in the apartment. We had to rough it for a few weeks until our new furniture arrived and the borrowed inflatable beds were replaced by the more conventional variety but, in general, things were going smoothly for once. As usual though, I did most of the organising whilst Tony slipped into a routine of going out for a pint or two in the afternoon. The only niggle was that he kept pestering me to arrange for the Internet to be connected. As I had lost my job a couple of weeks before the move, when the people who employed me disappeared and became un-contactable (the cowards still owe me €192.50 by the way), the Internet was not high on my list of priorities so I ignored him. We had had a satellite dish installed to avoid future problems with rebroadcast systems and so Homer and Hitler rejoined us much to Tony's delight, but the nagging about the Internet continued until I gave in and duly arranged a connection. I didn't know what his problem was, as there was a perfectly good Internet café close to his favourite watering hole, but eventually the modem arrived and I swear I had never seen him spring into action so quickly in all of the time I had known him. It was all a bit strange, but I thought nothing more of it. The apartment was cosy, and actually felt more like home than the villa ever had, but perhaps that had something to do with the fact that I was no longer worrying about things and was actually looking forward to a relaxing and stress free 2009. It was also nice to discover that, as the community had matured and settled, and people had come to accept the rules, even if they did not agree with them, life around the place had become far more laidback than it had been in the early days. People were generally less intrusive, we had a decent president and, compared with other communities nearby ours had turned out to be a good one.

Things continued to go well for us, and the exchange rate was in our favour in the last few days of November, so I transferred the villa money back to the UK. The scribbled receipt from my Spanish estate agent came in handy when I went to make the transfer, as the bank required proof that the cash had come from the proceeds of a legitimate property sale. The €25000 loss on the villa happily turned into a healthy £17500 profit upon the repatriation of the cash and I was happy with the transaction. Had I waited a couple of weeks longer I could have achieved a bit more, but I was not to know that at the time and I took my chance whilst I could.

Unfortunately, as things improved for us, life for Maisie took a significant downturn and she became a danger to herself. Still without the stimulation of television, her mental clarity deserted her and she began to struggle to carry out routine tasks. She took to wandering the streets at odd hours dressed in bizarre outfits, and we all had to admit that she could no longer cope with living on her own. As she was now in need of care rather than just charitable visits, her family had to decide whether they should put her into a retirement home in Spain or send her back to one in the UK. The difficulty was that English-speaking residential facilities for the elderly in Spain were looking very expensive, and in a Spanish-speaking establishment, she would be unable to communicate sufficiently even if any would agree to take her in. After considering her medical and financial issues, her relatives opted to fly her back to an old folk's home in the UK before she became unfit to travel. There is no doubt in my mind that the sudden withdrawal of any TV programming from her day speeded up what may have been an inevitable decline in mental capacity; the change in her was swift, dramatic, and extremely sad. I made one last visit to say goodbye, but I think she had already forgotten who I was and, for once, I was thankful for her memory loss; it prevented that last goodbye from becoming too emotional.

I had booked a flight for December 6th to return to Manchester for Christmas 2008, and Tony was to follow me a couple of weeks later (after I had done all of the shopping and bought all of the presents). I was to stay for a whole month and it was my first trip back since Christmas 2007. I was really looking forward to it – that is until I got up unusually late one morning and made a discovery that was to change the course of my life.

Tony had gone out. This didn't worry me as we had never lived in each other's pockets. On autopilot, I went into my morning ritual of brewing a cup of tea (to make myself feel relatively human) and heading towards the computer to check my e-mails. A whirring noise from the computer tower indicated that Tony had already had it on, and had forgotten to close it down properly when he had finished with it. His screen saver had kicked in and I waggled the mouse around to bring the system to life so that I could log him off. The screen saver fell away to reveal a picture of Tony, which would have been all right, had it *not* been a picture of Tony on an Internet dating website advertising himself as a 'Single male looking for 'fun', and a long term relationship'! My stomach did that thing that stomachs do when you go over a rise and fall in the road at speed. I couldn't believe what I was seeing! I stood there frozen to the spot, unblinking, with my mouth open and my morning cuppa hovering somewhere around chin level. The account had an e-mail facility attached to it and, of course, I went straight into it. It was clear that he had been arranging to meet people, and some of the mail he was receiving was, shall we say, quite graphic! What is more, the meetings coincided with his trips back to the UK to see his 'mum'! I made a note of his username (I knew what his password would be as he is not very inventive) before closing the screen and logging him off. I was absolutely stunned, but I tried to go about my usual business and appear normal, whilst trying to work out what to do next. Tony returned a few minutes later and went straight to the computer with a look of panic on his face, "Did I leave myself logged on?" he asked, anxiously. "You might have done," I replied calmly, "but the system had locked up so I just shut it all down. Why, will you have lost something important?" He looked instantly relieved, "No it's ok, I think I might have logged off anyway. What are we doing today...?"

When Tony went out for his pint as usual at 2pm, I immediately logged back on to the dating website with his username to read all his e-mails and print the juicier ones off (this had never been my style, and I did feel a bit guilty, but I'm not apologising either). I wanted to know what was going on, how long it had been going on for, and with *whom*. It was clear the flat in Manchester had been used to entertain at least two people, and that he had had other meetings in a Travel Lodge just outside Manchester – he even had a future date fixed up in South Wales to keep himself occupied over the Christmas period at his mother's! How bloody organised is that? I even found photographs of him with at least two other women; he had been shagging around like a hormonal teenager all the time I had been worried sick about him, his health, and our finances. Fucking Welsh bastard! (I know that this is not good sentence construction but I do not care).

I reasoned that if there was incriminating material stored on the computer in Spain, there was bound to be more on the computer in Manchester, where he had spent most of the time on his own during 2006. I decided to keep my mouth shut and act normal (it was not easy).

When December 6th finally arrived, I set off back to Manchester. Tony texted me saying "See you soon, I love you!" I resisted the urge to text back "Fuck off you unfaithful Welsh twat". The weather in Manchester was the same as it was in Spain; bright, crisp and dry. I enjoyed doing a small amount of Christmas shopping, met up with some friends, handed over the inevitable fag orders and began rounding off the book. I also got stuck into the computer and found more stuff relating to *another* dating website or Internet chat-room of some description dating back to 2002! The bastard had been screwing around for at least six bloody years - and *I* hadn't suspected a thing. By now, I knew that our relationship was completely over; the scale of the deception, the length of time it had been going on, and the number of people involved were just too much for anyone but a complete idiot to contemplate forgiving. I went around the flat packing his stuff up and transferring it to the car. When he went to see his 'mother' for Christmas he would not be coming back – and I would certainly be returning to Spain alone in the New Year. He was due back on December 18th. I continued to log into his profile and it was clear that his Internet activity had increased as soon as he knew I was safely out of the way. I showed John and Alex everything I had discovered and I was glad to see that they were as stunned as I had been. It made me feel a bit better because they had clearly not suspected him of anything either, and they had both known him for more than 10 years. I did a bit of crying, got on with my Christmas preparations, and waited for the 18th to arrive.

On December 11^{th,} Janet rang me with more bad news; her lovely mum had been found dead in bed in Los Montesinos that very morning. At a time when their mum should have been making her way to the UK for the holidays, Janet and her sisters were, instead, on their way out to Spain to attend her funeral. Janet's mum had loved Spain, and had been one of the few people I had met who had genuinely made exactly the right decision for themselves; she had enjoyed it for only two years. It was fortunate for her daughters that she had taken out one of the very popular funeral plans available; her wishes were clearly documented, and the company concerned organised everything so that it ran smoothly, taking the strain off the girls. The only delay they experienced was a wait of several days for a cremation certificate that would enable them to bring their mum home as hand luggage! Janet coped remarkably well and my fear that her mum's death would knock her right back down thankfully did not materialise (I think you can actually reach a stage when things stop affecting you because you are already at saturation point). I did not mention my problems with Tony and his antics; it could wait until another day.

Tony arrived back exactly one week later. I had had three weeks to come to terms with the situation and I had decided to remain calm and dignified. I had already done all my crying and my mind was made up. Our 17-year relationship had come to a sudden and upsetting end but I didn't want things to turn nasty, and there was no reason why they should. He was home for several hours before he began to notice that his personal possessions were missing. Eventually he said, "Where have you put my shaving stuff and my medication?" "It's all in the car for you to take to your mum's because you are leaving me tomorrow and our relationship is over," I replied, "I know what you've been up to so don't bother trying to talk your way out of it." He made a noise that was a cross between a sigh and a schoolboy snigger, "I thought you were on to me, but I wasn't sure. It was that day I left the computer on wasn't it?" I just nodded. There was no big bust up, no name-calling or finger pointing, just an air of disappointment and sadness. He left the next morning and my life felt empty. It was as if a big hand had come down from the sky armed with a duster and it had wiped out my future with a casual swish of its wrist.

I kept the news of the break up from my dad and brother. I wanted time to get my head together and the chance to return to Spain to decide what to do with my life without subliminal pressure from anyone else. I didn't want to cause my dad any anxiety and I didn't want to ruin our Christmas. I coped well under the circumstances and I eventually told my dad the following Easter when I was back on my feet and managing well on my own in Spain.

January 2009 To June 2010

I returned to Spain alone mid way through January 2009 without much of an idea of what I was going to do, or where I was going to end up. I consoled myself with the thoughts that I had the book to finish off and enough cash in the bank to support myself for the foreseeable future. Having learned from my previous mistakes, I resisted the temptation to make snap decisions, which I knew I would go back on within weeks.

I had the unpleasant task of explaining Tony's absence to our friends, and I also had to organise shipping his belongings back to Wales. We were communicating on a practical level and he kept indicating that if I would just forgive him he would never have another affair, but I just couldn't get over what had happened. I had accepted that I was single once more at the age of 46, and that I would either remain on my own or I would have to get back into the dating game. Neither option filled me with much excitement, and frankly, the prospect of finding a new partner amongst the geriatric population of the Costa Blanca was slim! Without anyone else to worry about, I just knuckled down and got on with normal life, such as it was.

As the weeks and months passed by almost unnoticed, my mood lifted and I finally found myself enjoying my life in Spain in the very way I had hoped for right at the beginning of the venture. I was coping well and getting out and about in my car, trying new things and exploring a bit. I lost weight and felt, confident, fit, and healthy for the first time in years.

It became apparent that the publisher I was signed up with was not hitting its timescales so I decided to cancel the contract and find another one. When I became restless, I would book a flight back to the UK and stay there for a couple of weeks until I felt better. Life was great.

The economy was still suffering and people seemed to be leaving Spain in droves. Most were going back for financial reasons, but some were unhappy with the changes to the healthcare rules for early retirees. More Spanish construction companies began to go into administration and the local press contained reports of increasing numbers of Brits worried about the deposits they had made on unfinished properties. For many people, years of legal wrangling could lie ahead, instead of the prospect of owning a dream home.

I continued to enjoy myself, unworried and unaffected by the problems going on around me. My opportunities for meeting new people however were limited as I made a conscious effort not to become involved with any group of people who regularly spent their days in a haze of alcohol. The drinking culture amongst retired Brits is a serious cause for concern, and I am aware that many previously 'social' drinkers have developed serious alcohol habits whilst whiling away their lives in the sun. Avoiding the problem came at a price socially, as there are few other places to meet someone new. However, I didn't want to be lumbered with a heavy drinker, so I had to accept the consequences of my decision.

And so to the present date…in 2010 the exodus continues, and property prices have gone through the floor. The canny Spaniards have begun to buy up the properties of fleeing expats at a fraction of their original prices. They must be laughing their socks off! (The bank that repossessed Janet's house has just sold on it to a Spanish family for a massive €125000 less than Janet and her husband paid for it back in 2005!)

Life is relaxed and stress free for me now, and time passes very quickly. The traumas of the first few years are behind me, and Spain is much more familiar and therefore much more like home. However, in the 18 months I have lived here alone none of my family or friends from the UK has been out to visit me and so I have been left wondering what Spain has to offer me now that my circumstances have changed. I did not come to Spain to be alone and I have no one to share my enjoyment with so, despite the fact that I am happy, it all seems quite pointless. Perhaps I will have to accept that the Spanish venture is over for me for the time being. I have recently met a great guy from Halifax so, almost 30 years after I left the area, my dad is keeping his fingers crossed and hoping to have me back in West Yorkshire very soon – and maybe I will be back on the trail of a decent estate agent once again.

Estate Agents

The problem with estate agents in Spain (apart from the fact that they *are* estate agents) is that they do not seem to have any standard operating practices. Their charges vary considerably from fixed rates to whatever they think they can get away with, and what is included in the cost also seems to be a bit vague. Go into any website and you will find an abundance of information for buyers, but if you want to sell there will be nothing published openly and the only facility available to you will be 'Contact us'. It is very frustrating. Personally, I cannot see the harm in a simple declaration such as *'Our selling fees start at €5000 and include accompanied viewings, translation, notary appointment, advice about documentation, changeover of utility bills, listing on our Internet website and display of your property in our office. We operate on a no win, no fee basis. For a personal valuation of your property and more information about our services and charges please ring...'* What's so hard about that?

The way things stand, there does not appear to be any industry regulation or standard and many of us don't fully understand what is going on, or who to trust. From a seller's point of view, I think it would be clearer if agents charged a percentage fee, and were sufficiently experienced to fairly, and accurately, put a market value on different types of property in particular areas. I tried to select agents who specialised in selling properties in one area as they developed local knowledge and had a clear idea of what would sell and how much it would sell for. Another requirement of mine was that they should have an office and have been trading in property in Spain for some years. The fly-by-night agents, which sprang up during the Spanish property boom, disappeared just as swiftly, and countless documents and keys went missing in the process. Now that times are hard it is clear that the 'good guys' have survived They do not hit their sellers with massive charges for flying time-wasting sightseers over to Spain and generally they are straightforward, competent and charge reasonable prices. They are prepared to discuss what their charges cover, and *when* costs are openly discussed, and reasonable, a certain element of suspicion is removed from the process. Some agents stipulate that sellers and buyers should never meet, and this, inevitably, leads to the belief that each side is being told something different. A good agent will ask a vendor what their position is, and advise them of quick, and not so quick, sale prices. They will also have learned to spot time-wasting 'buyers'; people who while away their time viewing properties they have no intention of buying. It is important that such people are weeded out of the process as they raise false hope for the seller and waste the agent's time. Decent photographs of the property are also important; I cannot believe the number of appalling illustrations displayed in agents' windows, and on property websites. Also a good agent should be used to dealing with customers from many different nationalities; as British buyers have all but disappeared over the horizon, the Finns, French and Russians have emerged as the nationalities that currently have the cash to buy. If an acceptable offer *is* made, you must ensure that a non-refundable deposit is secured as soon as possible, and a completion date agreed upon and put into a contract of sale.

As a buyer back in 2006, I discovered that agents generally made no differentiation between relocators, investors, and holiday-home purchasers. Each category of buyer has different needs and wants. The stress levels on relocators in particular is high; many have to juggle selling and moving out of their old UK home with taking possession of their new Spanish property. At the Spanish end, shifting timescales can make coordinating the move almost impossible, especially if you are waiting for the completion of a new build property. Our agents just did not seem to care and very little help was available. If you are accompanied by elderly relatives, children, or animals, well tough – that's your problem. A lot more assistance and understanding for individual circumstances would go a long way to improving the image of estate agents in Spain. Currently, we are all just the same old irritating customers in their 'one size fits all' scheme. The outcome is often that relocators have to face the additional costs associated with arranging storage for furniture, placing pets in kennels, and renting overpriced accommodation from the very agents who do not care about them.

Similarly, I do not believe that investors are correctly advised that Spanish property should be viewed as a risky, long term, investment and that a quick loss rather than a quick profit is far more likely to be the outcome of a purchase. I was dismayed to overhear an agent encouraging a young man to put his money into a Spanish property instead of a UK pension fund. These people are not industry-regulated financial advisors; when he gets a bad return he will have no comebacks. There is a new saying amongst expats in Spain 'If you want to end up with a small fortune in Spain you have to start out with a large one!' For thousands of people that sentiment is uncomfortably close to the truth.

There *are* decent, straightforward, and honest agents in Spain; unfortunately, the majority do not know who they are or where they are and so the process remains one of potluck. If you were intending to sell, my advice would be to ask around for personal recommendations; those who have recently sold a property are the best people to give such advice.

My first agent turned out to be worse than useless, and I laughed in his face when he asked me if I had bought as an 'investment'. I told him that my money would have been safer in a suitcase under the bed. The only communications I received from him were e-mails asking me if I wanted to reduce the price. I eventually sacked him after two price drops failed to secure any viewers, serious or not. During one of my meltdowns, I considered using a company who paid 'cash in 24 hours' for ridiculously under-priced properties just to get the apartment off my hands, and Tony suggested giving in to the system and putting both properties up with one of the big boys. Enquiries in July 2008 revealed that one 'international' company had reduced its commission charge from 18% to 10%, and two had gone out of business. I felt that 10% was still far too much, and I eventually sold the villa via a local Spanish agent who only charged 3%. Consider your agent as a partner, co-operate, and work with them to achieve your goals. If you pick the right agent for your property and are sensible about pricing it for the current market (whatever that might be at the time) you will attract viewers. If you don't, your property will become just another sun-faded photograph in the agent's window, and the 'For Sale' sign will be up for a very long time.

On Reflection

The truth is that, in 2010, more Brits are leaving Spain than are arriving, and lots more would like to go if only they could. Statistics indicate that, even in a relatively stable economic climate, two thirds of people habitually return to their country of origin within the first three years. I agree. Within those first couple of years there seems to exist a pain barrier that has to be experienced before you are fully aware of what you have let yourself in for. As I approach the end of year five, I know that the worst of it is over, and how long I stay is now more up to me than the influence of external factors. Property companies and TV shows don't highlight the scale of the failure rate, and so new buyers are kept in blissful ignorance and believe that the venture works out marvellously for the majority of those who take the chance. Pauline once asked me if I wished I had done things differently and I had to stop myself from saying "You could have warned me that moving to Spain was almost a one-way street and that I would have a hard time reselling and getting out of the country." I'm sure that until she tried to sell her own property, she didn't appreciate how hard it was. I have grown fond of Spain but yes, if I am honest, there were times when I wished we had just rented somewhere. However, I am a strong believer in things happening for a reason, and I think I was meant to have this experience because it will do me some good later in life. I also hope this book helps others to avoid making the same mistakes.

The best advice I can give is rent, rent, rent, until you know what you are doing. Don't make the move lightly; if you find you don't like it and you are only renting you can pack up and go home quickly and easily. If you buy off-plan, as I did, you will be stuck for some time and you are very likely to lose money if you cannot stick it out. I was lucky that the exchange rate moved in my favour and I made a small profit. Janet lost the lot. Pauline intended to remain in Spain as a renter to retain some flexibility; it didn't last long – she now lives on the east coast – of England. Those who *would* buy again say they would choose resale over new-build.

There is no getting away from the fact that there are many unhappy people stuck in Spain who would love to go home, but who are unable to owing to the lack of available finances. There must be millions of euros tied up in unwanted and unloved Spanish properties. Property prices have clearly dropped throughout Europe and finance is much harder to raise. This, coupled with the poor pound to euro exchange rate, has resulted in Spanish property losing its ability to attract UK-based purchasers. As far back as 2007, lending on mortgages for Spanish properties was down by 10% and interest in new-build properties was abating to such an extent that the builders were freezing their prices and abandoning half-built developments. By the end of 2007, builders were actually offering large discounts in order to offload unwanted stock. At the beginning of 2008, some big Spanish constructors were in real difficulty (when San Jose went into administration, it hit the front pages of the Spanish press) and at least two large agents had more or less gone out of business. Lord knows what has happened to the deposits held by these companies. Before she became a casualty herself, Pauline said that certain constructors' new developments had been dropped from the agents' brochures, as completion could not be guaranteed. Resale properties have now become the more attractive, and safer, option.

There is also no doubt that Spanish properties have become much harder to sell, (especially since the eastern European property markets have opened up) and they are *not* good short-term investments no matter what anyone says. Taxes are high and it would be wise to take tax advice based on your personal circumstances, rather than to buy a book full of general examples, to be clear what you are paying for and why. I used to pay a solicitor to be my fiscal representative and there were times when money disappeared from my account and I was not *exactly* sure what it had paid for. I would never have put up with the situation in the UK, but for some strange reason I did in Spain. After selling the villa, I took control of my own tax payments and so far I have managed to sort everything out myself.

I doubt that the British love affair with Spain will ever die off completely. Geographically, it is well placed for short-haul, cheap flights (though even the price of these has increased as airlines charge extra for baggage, meals, etc), but there is no doubt that many potential customers have been put off by the poor exchange rate and the economic crisis. I would advise anyone to opt for a resale property in an area that has already been completed and had its habitation certificates issued by the local town hall. As Spanish building companies struggle to pay their loans for land purchases, some developments have been abandoned and left unfinished; such sites are dangerous and are unlikely to be connected to the services.

If the market ever recovers, the country would do well to rid itself of the dodgy practices countenanced within the property-selling communities right through from the local councils and notaries to the builders and estate agents. Honest people investing their retirement funds should be able to buy knowing that all transactions have been carried out correctly and within the law and that they have some degree of timely protection if things should go wrong. Taking years to sort out disputes whilst people are denied access to property they have paid for is just not acceptable. An article in the local press published in September 2007 declared that the authorities intended to begin clamping down on the 'black money' practice of making a portion of the payment for a property in cash; thus avoiding the payment of tax on the whole amount due. The article annoyed me because foreign buyers of Spanish property were not the people who invented this scam, yet it seemed that the warning was directly aimed at such people. The practice is actually ingrained in the system, and is difficult to avoid. People go along with it because they are constantly reassured that 'this is how things are done in Spain'. So it is accepted as part of the unfathomable make-up of Spain, and it is the Spanish system that allows it to continue unchecked. Despite the declaration, in 2010, it is still going on.

Luckily, we had no real traumas with our purchases, other than those created by the very agents who were supposed to be helping us. The properties were legally and soundly built (even if there were no true 90 degree corners in the villa) and a potential serious loss of cash was averted owing to the financial meltdown in the UK.

Equally, I was relatively satisfied with the income from the rental of the apartment and having it provided me with something to do in those very difficult early months when I was alone. The commitment of the holiday bookings forced me to remain and get on with the job at a time when I would have otherwise lacked the strength to stay. There is no doubt that the biggest problem we faced was Tony's collapse in November 2005 and the ripple effect that that had throughout the following 12-month period. We got off to a bad start with the Spanish venture and what was supposed to be a joint adventure turned into a lonely slog for me, and a year of frustration for him. Arguments were caused because we ended up poles apart on how we viewed the experience. The impact of health issues had not occurred to either of us, and by the time it did, it was too late.

Had we been together as planned, we may have been much happier from the word go, but we still would have reached a stage where we had to accept that the trial period was up and that a firm decision had to be taken as to where we wanted to be long-term. One of the greatest difficulties arises when couples find themselves in a position where one of them is far happier than the other. The dynamic of the relationship changes and you see different sides to each other that you never knew existed. If a relationship was under strain prior to the move, differences in perception can bring the whole thing to a head. There is no doubt that, despite all your best attempts at forward planning, you eventually have to take the plunge and experiment a bit to discover how you truly feel about a situation, and you will never know how you *are* going to feel until you try it. As it was, we were always in a position where I had been in Spain a year longer than Tony, and inevitably, my experiences were very different from his. I associated the villa with one of the most difficult years of my adult life and consequently, I ended up having very little love for it as a home and wanted to be rid of it because of what it represented. Tony continued for a long time to view it as a beautiful property with a lot of potential. The tedium of living on an urbanisation eventually united us on the issue of selling it; not finances, or a problem with the property itself.

There may always be a subconscious thought of a return to the UK floating around somewhere in my mind, waiting to make itself felt during a negative moment. However, I also feel that, as more time passes, going back becomes less of an option. I have already had an adverse reaction to returning to life and work in Manchester, so Spain has clearly affected me more than I had appreciated. It would be nice to think that any of us could go forward or backwards with total impunity, but we don't live in a bubble and there are always going to be people around who will judge your actions, and the thought of this inevitably impacts on your decision-making. I once would have said that *I* would not be growing old here, but now I am not so sure.

Fate interfered with our well-made plans and I think that happens to many who are brave enough to try living their dream. I have still not completely unravelled the mess that resulted from Tony's collapse in 2005, but I can't turn the clock back. Those circumstances forced me to keep the flat in Manchester at a time when I would rather have sold it, and consequently it became hard for me to stop thinking of the UK as home and this affected my ability to adjust. Of course now, and with much hindsight, it has been fortuitous to be able to keep a foothold in the UK as I can now return if I want to, and am not trapped in Spain as many people are.

So do I now have any regrets? I have been asked countless times if I regret the move or conversely if I would recommend it. Well I do have *some* regrets, but it is pointless wasting any more time and energy dwelling on them. I have to deal with the situation as it currently stands and get on with my life as it is now. Equally, I would *never* go so far as to recommend it, but nor would I go out of my way to discourage someone who was certain about what they were doing. I think everyone should make up his or her own mind based upon their own circumstances and not use anyone else as a benchmark. I think Tony and I were seeking freedom from something from which we could never truly escape. I have come to terms with that now and my mindset has changed. I have survived somehow but it has not been a laugh-a-minute, and it has not been a dream existence. I am so glad we never hooked up as reps with the property company because I would hate to think that we had sold a concept that doesn't really exist to someone. I have seen many people go home quickly and know that a large number of decent people will continue to be sadly let down by the process. Even many of those who 'make it' and stay, harbour disappointments, but when you are feeling OK these things don't tend to be mentioned. Pauline always says she never told anyone a lie when she was selling property, and I believe her because I know that she is a good person, but I also know that there is a difference between telling lies and being open with the facts. Omitting to tell people things that would be to their benefit is almost as bad in my opinion. When we met Pauline and Phil, they were novices in the selling game and I believe that their company trained them to offer up only certain information; they literally did not *have* all the facts to give us.

Our move was motivated by a desire to try for a better life, and perhaps we over-romanticised it. Our lives ended up far from the simple and uncomplicated ones we had hoped for, and unfortunate turns of event forced us to focus on vital issues far too late in the game. Some people, no doubt, do take to their 'new life' like a duck to water, but when you deliberately strip your life of all that is familiar, the result can be simultaneously very liberating and very destabilising. Whatever happens, you have to try not to judge yourself too harshly. Do what you have to do with grace and enthusiasm and try to enjoy the moment (I will be the first to admit that this is damned hard when you feel dreadful). There will be times when you feel that your life has descended into hopeless chaos, but you will have to accept that the upheaval of the move will be inconsistent and uncomfortable at times. Try to be philosophical; as they say in the films, "Shit happens". By facing up to things and forcing yourself to make rational decisions you can regain control and get your situation back into some sort of reasonable perspective. There have been times when I felt nothing but total despair, and when you are experiencing that level of emotional pain the prospect of any kind of relief is better than nothing at all. At such times you need to remind yourself how long it took you to organise your arrival in Spain and, if at all possible, you should spend at least the same amount of time and effort planning your departure. If you don't, you will lose out financially and compound your problems even further. There is an abundance of pond life out here silently waiting to pick up the spoils of your hasty surrender; house clearance firms, chaps who buy cars for cash; property speculators who specialise in buying up houses at a fraction of their true value, and of course the estate agents. I was dismayed to see an advertisement on a leaflet for a company named something similar to 'Suicidal Sales Dot Com', aimed at the desperate seller. The wording 'bank repossessions and distress sales' is increasingly cropping up in literature and advertisements; it highlights the situation many are in. The banks are becoming impatient with those people who fail to address their financial problems, believing that they can just throw the keys back at the bank and walk away. The tactic no longer works and if a bank fails to recoup the cost of a mortgage at auction then they now take steps to track down the previous owner for payment of the balance. It is clear that people chasing something that does not exist – a *guaranteed* good life in the sun – are wasting a lot of money on overseas properties, and ending up in a financial hole. It is important to remain realistic about your circumstances and not to enter an *Emperor's New Clothes* mindset whereby everyone else can see that you are heading for disaster and you fail to acknowledge it in order to save face. If all the joy and wonder has gone out of your new life, it is brave to admit defeat and call it a day. Acknowledge what you have gained from the experience and move on; those who were brave enough to try once will be brave enough to try again.

Outwardly, men seem to cope with the upheaval far better than women do. Men therefore invariably write the amusing, anecdotal books, though I suspect that they often only see the funny side much later and their wives would recall a different version of the same events. Some situations that I can laugh about now had me tearing my hair out when they were actually happening. Women tend to worry more about finances and the people they have left behind, and are more likely to experience emotional extremes. There will be times when there is nothing fun or relaxing about your new life, and as well as being haunted by the old one you will not be convinced that anything much has changed. If you make the move as part of a family group or a couple, don't be surprised if, at the beginning, you drive each other crazy. Living with a loved one 24/7, and not having a new circle of friends to break the monotony will put a strain on the strongest of relationships. Equally, if your relationship is already under strain don't believe for one minute that 'getting away from it all' will be a magic solution and that everything will suddenly be hunky-dory. On the contrary, cracks will soon become chasms and what might have been redeemable before the move will become irreparable after it – and one if not both of you will want to do a runner and consequently you may lose everything (just ask Janet).

I wouldn't want to create the impression that it has all been bad, or discourage anyone from pursuing their own dream. Most of my writing has been done when I felt dire, simply because I needed to catch the mood of the moment. I have had some good times and I have met some nice people. I have made some great friends and had experiences I would never have had within my narrow employment and social circle back in Manchester. Ultimately, the move has served its purpose now and I feel the urge to get on with the next phase of my life becoming stronger. The whole thing has been very cathartic; and I am now at a crossroad that will take me well into the future, I just have to choose the right direction. I am glad to be out of the rut, but it has been a difficult transition to make and I would rather not go through anything like it ever again. The best way I can describe it is as an upsy-downsy experience; very much like the roller coaster analogy I used at the beginning – periods of exhilaration changing places quickly with periods of despair. It has been a challenging time but I now feel that it has been the making of me in many ways. To stick with the unsatisfactory just because it was safe and familiar would have been to rob myself of the chance to reach my full potential. In a way I was in a prison of my own making back in the UK; I got out of it and survived. I will not now stick with another situation with which I am not totally at ease (and I am convinced that many people do exactly that just to save face). I have found that my interest in new things has increased, and I am now more open to suggestions and can see myself doing something very different from that which I have been programmed to do over the past 20-odd years. I truly believe that struggle is nature's way of strengthening and too many of us go out of our way to avoid changes to our comfort level. What doesn't kill you *does* make you stronger and I have gained so much despite the traumas.

I know now that too much free time really does not suit me and I look forward to the prospect of working in some capacity, but preferably on my own terms. Some of us are destined to work, and not working has not agreed with me. What I hope for in the future is work that allows for some personal growth and a sense of satisfaction throughout the day. I don't want to be a wage slave again and I don't want to put my happiness on hold until 5pm each day. I think I have a clearer idea of where I am going in life and, in some ways, I feel quite refreshed. I have had the time to look at various employment opportunities and wish that I had had that freedom when I was much younger – I may well have made a better initial choice for myself, but there are now several options open to me that I feel very excited about. It is a privilege to be free enough to alter your life path and in that respect, I am very fortunate. I am lucky to have supportive family and friends and without them, I would never have survived. I appreciate those close to me far more than I ever did when I was too busy to pay them the right amount of attention. I have learned a great deal from the Spanish about family values and feel that this is an area of my life that has been enriched by the whole experience. Once again, I am fortunate enough to have undergone this enlightenment whilst my dad is still alive and I will have the opportunity to be there for him in his old age. The acid test of any relationship is its ability to survive when one partner is going through a crisis. Tony never really appreciated my sense of urgency, and I never really understood his lack of concern over our situation. Our break up was not caused by the situation in Spain and I do wish I had found out what was going on before the move. However, that is another important lesson learned; no matter where you go in the world to live your dream, the problems associated with normal, everyday life will still follow you

If Janet had written this book the outcome at this point would have been so different, and that makes me feel very lucky indeed. Whilst I have actually 'lost' very little, her entire life has been torn apart. She is not even just right back where she started – financially she is in a far worse position and she may never fully recover. Janet's story is a tragedy and, though she may be an extreme example, I know that she is by no means an isolated case. She is slowly getting her life back in order, and she insists that she will return to Spain one day to live her dream the way she wanted to in the beginning, but deep down I doubt that she will ever be able to view the place so positively a second time. I sincerely hope that she finds satisfaction on her own doorstep and forgets about returning on a permanent basis, at least until her son has completed his education.

I have yet to meet anyone who is totally happy with who they are, or with the way their life has turned out, wherever they live. We all have our traumas, but I would advise anyone to sit down and really analyse their issues and get to the root of their problems before they decide that the solution is to move to another country. For example, if you hate your job try just changing it; if you hate your neighbours, just move locally. Leaving your country of birth and all the familiarity of a lifetime that goes with it is a drastic step. Try taking a long holiday, go part-time at work, take a career break, train to do something different. Exhaust your options at home before you throw in the towel and move abroad. There is an old Chinese proverb which says, "To know the road ahead, ask those who are coming back". It is good advice; you can learn a lot from the mistakes of others and that is the purpose of this book. Spain is a great country, but you have to have sufficient resources and make a big effort to fit in.

Remember, no one should move purely for the weather because it quite simply is not enough. If you take the sun out of the equation, ask yourself what you are left with other than life in a country where you don't speak the language.

Generally, things are fine when all is going well but as soon as you hit a hurdle, the communication issue is something you really have to face up to. In winter, the houses can be bitterly cold and the weather even more miserable than at home. We were unaware of the dampness in one room of our villa until I moved the bed one day and discovered mould on the edge of the mattress. In summer, many people find the heat in July and August totally overpowering and the place is overrun with tourists. Living and working in Spain is far more difficult than holidaying in, or retiring to it. Which group do you fit into? Can you survive? Can you earn enough to meet your financial commitments? Do you have a job lined up? Do you have enough money to start your own business? The state of the pound has taken many by surprise and several of my retired neighbours are living hand to mouth from one month to the next. Some have had to take jobs working long hours for little pay to make ends meet.

Everyone should think ahead to how they will cope and what they will do if their partner becomes seriously ill or dies. I have seen the health of at least six people deteriorate significantly whilst I have been here, and five people known to me have died. If things are not put in place for such an eventuality, people find themselves struggling with a system they don't fully understand, at a time when they are grieving (and anxious about their own futures alone in Spain). If a person dies in Spain, his or her bank account is frozen very quickly. Therefore, if you arrive as a couple, it is sensible to ensure you each have a separate account holding emergency funds so that the surviving partner is not left without access to cash. Before the property of the deceased can be sold, the remaining partner may be liable for inheritance tax, and prior to marketing, the name of the deceased may have to be removed from the deeds (one elderly acquaintance had to wait 18 months for the land registry to complete this action). It is a complex legal area, so it is necessary to take the correct advice from a professional. Organising your affairs <u>before</u> you die will make sorting out your estate much easier for the loved ones you leave behind. Janet's mum saved her daughters a lot of heartache by planning ahead and purchasing a funeral plan, which was valid in both the UK and mainland Spain. Following her example, I have since done the same myself.

The sad fact is that many people do not feel catered for in the UK any longer and have the urge to escape. We do not have a society in which everyone is able to feel comfortable. It is hard to equate the UK of today with the one that passionately fought wars in the defence of its own freedom and identity. It seems now to simply roll over and accept increasingly harebrained and divisive politically correct ideas from the European Union. I have heard Brits in Spain say that they would rather be strangers in Spain than strangers in their own country. It is a viewpoint I do not share, but one I do understand. It is hard to defend a country that criminalises people for putting rubbish in the wrong bin, yet ignores antisocial behaviour until some unfortunate victim is kicked to death on his own doorstep. It is difficult to comprehend the obsession with terrorism, identity cards and intrusion into the privacy of the general population, when care for the elderly, timely operations, availability of dental care, efficient collection of rubbish and decent public transport have a greater effect on the average person. Tony and I did not come to Spain because we hated the UK, but many people do, and these are the issues that they focus upon (one chap now refers to England as 'Bin-land').

I now sympathise far more with immigrants who feel that their only option for a decent life is to move to a country where their ability to communicate is far below that of their mother tongue. Many immigrants are intelligent, well-educated people and I believe that, given sufficient choices and opportunities in their homelands, most would prefer not to move. To be greeted with racism in their country of choice must be totally devastating – the transition is hard enough. I am aware that there is an element of the Spanish population who would prefer it if *we* were not *here*. One local playground displays graffiti declaring in Spanish "No English – Spanish zone only." I am sure that the only reason there has not been a reaction to it is that most Brits do not have a clue what it says.

I have gained a lot from my emotional turmoil even though experiencing it was truly awful. I now have a different attitude towards money and material things and care more about my family and friends. I neither want, nor need, a fancy job with a big salary, huge responsibilities, or pressure. I have many good things in my life and I have learned to be satisfied with them. I try harder to keep things in perspective and overall I hope I am a better human being. But, perhaps my biggest gain is that I have a greater appreciation for my homeland. It is not so bad, it is very tolerant, and it is a place I know, understand, and feel safe within. It may not be in the sun for the majority of the year, but it is a decent place to be and maybe (if I can ever sell the apartment) I will be back one day.

Franco was right; there are some things that only time can solve. Who knows what the future has in store?

One thing is certain though; I have decided that, from now on, *every* year is going to be *my* year.

The End

Lightning Source UK Ltd.
Milton Keynes UK
UKOW050155101211

183522UK00001B/13/P